YOU'RE UNDER
ARREST
I'M NOT KIDDING

THE TRIALS AND TRIBULATIONS
OF A
RELUCTANT COP

DON PARKER

CAROLDON BOOKS
PENSACOLA, FLORIDA

First Printing December 1988   5,000
Second Printing December 1989   10,000

Caroldon Books
1075 Farmington Road
Pensacola, Florida 32504

Printed in the United States of America

ISBN 0-9620073-1-5

This book is respectfully dedicated
to the memory of my brothers

DEPUTY DON COOK
DEPUTY DOUG HEIST
DEPUTY BUDDY RAY
DEPUTY CHARLIE WILKERSON
CORPORAL ERIC STREETER
PATROLMAN AMOS CROSS
PATROLMAN CURTIS JONES
PATROLMAN STEVE TAYLOR

who died while doing their duty and to

DEPUTY JIMMY ROOK

The bravest man I ever knew. He lost his battle with
cancer but his magnificent courage was an inspiration
to all who worked with him.

ACKNOWLEDGEMENTS

Getting a book out is an incredibly complex task and would not have been possible without the assistance of many people. Most authors seem to have a compulsion to thank every person who took the time to read the title. I am no exception.

First, I would like to thank former Sheriff Royal Untreiner, who had the foresight to hire me back in 1970. In a way, he truly made this book possible. Next, is Sheriff Vince Seely, who continued to promote me in spite of the doubts we both had.

Carolyn Cooper was more than just a print broker; she was a true partner, assisting in every facet of this project, even doing some of the proof reading. Frances Dunham agreed to take on the dual chores of artist and typographic designer. That's her watercolor on the cover and her vast artistic talent is evident throughout. She also volunteered to help with the copy editing (God bless her) and discovered 1642 errors in grammar, punctuation and spelling. Curt Shields of Curt Shields Photography did all the camera work, including the shot from which Frances made the watercolor. Sergeant Lee Wasdin, homicide investigator with the Escambia County Sheriff's Department, posed as the bad guy for the cover and was very convincing. The typesetting was handled by my friend Smitty at Southeastern Press in Mobile, Alabama and he was extremely helpful.

I must mention the contribution made by Eileen Klug of Astro-Graphics in Gulf Breeze, Florida, who convinced me to do it all myself. She gave me the confidence to launch out into the deep in spite of my nervousness.

To my mother, Sallie Smith, my father, Doug Parker, my brothers, Roger and Bob, my sister, Kathy, to Mark O'Brien and my other friends and co-workers who offered encouragement and constructive criticism, I say thank you all.

Finally, there is the enormous contribution of my wife, Carol. Without her loving support, unbelievable patience, and constant nagging, this book would just be another manuscript gathering dust on a closet shelf. She, more than anyone, made this book a reality. She is the light of my life and all I ever wanted.

INTRODUCTION

The stories you are about to read are all true, but I cheerfully admit I have used a few fictitious names, changed some locations and adjusted the chronology for a better flow. I also cleaned up the language. A lot.

While these adjustments were done for reasons of privacy, there is another consideration: Many of the deputies who appear in this book are still employed by the Escambia County Sheriff's Department. Many are crack shots and, because I wanted to be around to write a sequel, I felt it best to disguise certain facts.

I have tried to present a side of my profession rarely seen by the average citizen, whose knowledge of law enforcement comes mainly from television, movies or an occasional traffic ticket. While these are my stories, almost any cop can relate incidents just as entertaining and just as terrifying. The problem is getting them to open up. Cops are a clannish sort and most are reluctant to talk shop with people outside the profession, who might not understand that in tragedy there can be humor, and the job, which seems so full of action, is often downright monotonous.

We also don't like to admit that frequently our greatest heroes were simply in the right place at the right time, doing what they were paid to do. Heroes they may be, but the chances are any other cop would have done the same thing.

CONTENTS

1

THE EDUCATION
OF A ROOKIE

He pulled the black sweater over his head, fitting the snug collar to his thick neck. Adjusting the woolen cap, he stepped back to check his reflection in the mirror. At 6' 5" and 245 pounds, he seemed to fill the narrow room. Dressed in dark clothing from head to toe, he looked like a massive shadow. He glanced at his watch. Time to go.

Humming to himself he lifted the edge of the mattress. Picking up the heavy .45 automatic, he tucked it into his waistband and pulled the sweater over it. Still humming, he flipped off the light and left the room. Anthony Wesley was going to work.

Wesley enjoyed his "night work," as he called it, a lot more than his regular job. He spent his days at a linen plant, tossing hundred-pound bundles of dirty sheets off the incoming trucks. Solid as an oak, he shrugged off the killing labor and the stifling heat. Actually, he didn't mind the job that much. The pay wasn't bad, and he had several friends at the plant.

He had been a part-time burglar for the past three years. He figured he had started because of anger more than anything else. One evening, after losing ten dollars at the pool table to the bar owner, he retired to his beer, convinced he had been hustled. He brooded for a while and, after several more beers, resolved to do something about it. He returned to the deserted bar an hour after it closed, determined to get his money back.

Using a tire tool, he forced the flimsy door and, once inside, went after the jukebox and the coin-operated pool table. He didn't really know what he was doing, almost destroying the machines before he got them open.

He was so frightened as he labored in the darkness, the sweat ran off him in streams, but it was worth it. He walked off with nearly $300. He also felt a wild sense of exhilaration at what he had done. It was almost better than sex.

As the weeks went by, he started hitting other small bars and became quite proficient at popping the machines. Now it usually only took just a few seconds to get them open. He sometimes made an extra haul when he managed to find the bartender's hiding place for the day's receipts. They all seemed to use the beer cooler or the stock room. He guessed that over the years he had stolen thousands of dollars.

He smiled ruefully as he drove through the dark streets in his battered ten-year-old Buick. He wished he had managed to hold onto some of that money.

On the other side of town the rookie had almost finished dressing. He, too, spent some time in front of the mirror, admiring the view. His tailored deputy sheriff's uniform fit his lanky frame perfectly. Out of recruit school only three months, each day was still an adventure. With a last glance at the mirror, he carefully placed the cowboy-style straw hat on his head and walked out the door.

He arrived at the jail early, a sure sign of a rookie, and entered the bedlam of the muster room. Smoke-hazed and slightly sour-smelling, it was painted a dismal institutional green and furnished with battered, loose-jointed desk-chairs, the kind used in schools. Here roll was taken, work assignments made, and information passed along. At this hour the room was filled with milling deputies, waiting for muster to begin.

The noise, the bantering, the continual good-natured cursing, like background music in a department store, made it a scene familiar to law enforcement officers everywhere. Deputies in neatly pressed uniforms, badges gleaming, faces pink from recent shaves, smelling of soap and cologne, trooped into the room. They talked easily, laughing and joking, looking fresh and eager. There was no doubt they were the oncoming shift.

Their appearance was in strong contrast to the deputies of the off-going shift. These men had just worked the 3:00 P.M. to 11:00 P.M. shift, usually the busiest of the day, and they looked it. Their uniforms were wrinkled and sweat-stained, some dusty or muddy, others missing buttons or torn, showing hard usage at the hands of reluctant, but now incarcerated, suspects. The shadow of emerging stubble and the slightly haggard look to the faces was faintly reminiscent of combat troops coming off the line, which is exactly what they were.

The rookie enjoyed the noisy camaraderie of the muster room. The veterans made him suffer because of his transparent eagerness, but he laughed it off. He knew he was slowly being accepted.

So far it had been a busy midnight shift, and he was pleased to find he would be working the Warrington district again tonight. It was a busy area, full of bars and bottle clubs. Already this week he had handled a dozen fights two stabbings and had made five arrests. Activity slowed after the bars closed, but he filled the time checking buildings for burglaries.

Muster completed, he loaded his gear into his cruiser car and headed for his patrol district.

Several miles away, Anthony Wesley sat in his car a block from the Gizmo Bar. The usual crowd of plant workers, roofers, off-shore oil workers, and the recently jobless, drinking up their unemployment checks, had left early this evening.

When everyone had departed, Wesley left his car and approached the darkened building. Inserting the end of his tire tool at the edge of the door, he used a steady twisting motion to force the door away from the frame until it popped open. He slipped inside.

The jukebox was something of a disappointment, containing less than $10. He did better with the pool tables, dumping almost $50 into the cloth sack he used to hold the change. Checking behind the beer kegs, he felt a surge of excitement as his fingers touched the bank bag. They never learned.

He retrieved it from the hiding place but found only $17 in it. Still, it wasn't bad pay for ten minutes work. Walking out from behind the counter, he pulled a handful of pretzel bags from a rack. Scooping a cold beer from the cooler, he sat down to enjoy a snack at the bar.

It was warm in the cruiser car, and the vinyl seat was damp with sweat. The rookie twisted and squirmed, trying to ease the discomfort. So far, it had been quiet. He had made no arrests.

Just after 3:00 A.M. he turned into the parking lot of the Gizmo Bar. At first it appeared secure, but, as the headlights passed across the door, something caught his eye. The door looked as though it was not fully closed. Also, were those fresh pry marks on the door frame?

He stepped from the car, excitement rising in him. Policy required him to call for a backup unit, but he hated to do this if it was going to be a false alarm. He could imagine what the veterans would say about that! Besides, if someone was inside and he caught them all by himself, those veterans would really sit up and take notice of him.

He walked toward the door. The pry marks were definitely fresh. His heart started hammering as he unsnapped his holster and drew his revolver. He decided he would kick the door open and jump inside, holding his flashlight away from his body as he had been taught in rookie school. He raised his knee, aiming his foot at the door. This was it!

Wesley had almost finished his little meal when the glare of headlights splashed across the wall. He slid off the bar stool and moved in a crouch to the window. He pulled the bulky forty-five from his belt and thumbed the safety off. Peering through the dusty venetian blinds, he saw a car come to a halt in the parking lot. A spotlight flared and, swiveling slowly, centered on the door. A figure stepped from the car and walked toward the building, a star gleaming on his chest. It was a deputy.

Wesley left the window and eased to the door, his weapon ready. When it opened, he would shoot through it; the thin wood should be no obstacle for the heavy slugs. Footsteps crunched on the oyster shell parking lot. He tensed, finger firm on the trigger.

The rookie stared at the door for long seconds, a faintly comical figure, his leg upraised as though to mount a horse. A strange sensation passed through him, one he had never experienced before. It was pure fear.

He could not believe how afraid he was. His knees were jerking and twitching, his mouth was powder-dry, and his heart seemed to be trying to beat its way out of his chest. There was something inherently menacing about this place. He knew he could not go through that door alone.

He lowered his leg and backed slowly to his cruiser, the weakness in his legs making him stagger like a drunk. He collapsed into the front seat and, with sweat-slick fingers, picked up the microphone.

He tried to speak, but no sound emerged. He tried again and finally managed to croak, "109 to headquarters."

"Go ahead, 109."

Fighting the flutter in his voice, he said, "Send me a backup to the Gizmo Bar at Barrancas and Jamison; I've got an open door."

The rookie sat in his car for some minutes trying to get his breathing under control, as the dispatcher began sending other units to his location. After what seemed a very long time, he heard the comforting wail of sirens in the distance.

Inside the bar Wesley listened in disbelief as the footsteps receded from the door. The dude was going back to his car. Relief flooded through him. He was going to come out of this thing smelling like a rose! He would wait until the cop left, then head for his car with the money.

The minutes passed, but the cruiser did not leave. What the hell was going on? Then he heard the rising crescendo of approaching sirens and spat a curse. The pig had been calling for help. He had only one chance now. Jerking the door open, he vaulted into the glare of the headlights.

Just as the first backup unit arrived, the rookie saw the door to the bar fly open and a huge, black shape leap out and disappear around the corner of the building. It had happened so fast, he couldn't even draw his gun. He ran toward the rear of the Gizmo and heard the other deputy yell, "FREEZE, MISTER!"

He rounded the corner and saw a man dressed entirely in black spread against the wall, the other deputy's .38 pointing at his back.

They placed Wesley in the back of the rookie's cruiser with some difficulty. He was so big it was hard to squeeze him into the small space.

More deputies arrived, followed by the sergeant. Filled with euphoria now that it was over, the rookie wished he had gone ahead and tried to take the guy by himself.

One of the veterans called his name. The rookie walked over and saw he was shining his flashlight at something in the weeds. He looked down, and his heart lurched. His head swam dizzily, and for a moment he thought he would be sick.

There on the ground, obviously discarded by the fleeing burglar, was the heavy automatic, gleaming malevolently in the glare of the flashlight, the hammer still cocked. Ashen-faced, the rookie walked slowly back to his car.

That happened a long time ago, but I want to thank you, Anthony Wesley, for not shooting me that night. You taught me several important lessons, but the most important was the meaning, and the necessity, of fear.

2

THE CASE OF THE STOLEN BASEBALL CARDS

When I was growing up, I never wanted to be a cop; I wanted to be a fireman.

I was raised in the small town of Hartsdale, New York, an affluent bedroom community in Westchester County, some 20 miles from New York City. In our town we had a small cadre of trained firemen who maintained the equipment, drove the fire engines, and trained the volunteers who made up the bulk of the department.

When a fire call came in, the horn on top of the firehouse would go off in a coded sequence indicating the location of the call box nearest the fire. The paid firemen would drive the trucks to the scene, and all the volunteers who could get free would jump in their cars and tear off to the fire. As might be expected, there was a great deal of rushing around, screeching of tires, and yelling and cursing by the volunteers, all of whom were trying to get to the proper location.

Of course, we kids were vastly impressed by this barely controlled chaos. During daylight hours, if out of school, we leaped on our bikes and headed for the fire, praying we would arrive to find several houses engulfed in flames.

The firehouse drew me like a magnet, particularly on weekends when the weather was nice. The trucks were usually outside then being waxed and polished, and I was always begging for some job that would let me get close to the equipment. While never actually allowed to wax the trucks, occasionally I was afforded the rare privilege of scrubbing tire marks off the concrete floor or washing the mud and soot from the hoses after a brush fire.

Dizzy with gratitude at being entrusted with such awesome responsibility, I worked like a demon. While I was covering myself with dirt and ashes from the hoses, I could only think sadly of my friends who were not so lucky. They were compelled to play ball, climb trees, or ride their bikes, while I was having the time of my life.

I never could understand why they didn't seem more impressed when, bursting with self-importance, I would try to tell them of the huge thrill I had experienced cleaning filthy hoses or scrubbing the firehouse floor.

Yes, I worshipped firemen. Policemen, on the other hand, were rather remote figures. Since Hartsdale was not a big city, we did not have much day-to-day contact with cops. About all we had was the occasional traffic accident, seen while riding with our parents. We would be waved around the wreck by an impatient cop while we looked, goggle-eyed, for bloody bodies. Sometimes we would see a marked cruiser go by, lights flashing, or hear the far-off wail of a siren late at night, but that was about the extent of our contact with cops.

We saw a lot more of firemen, because they spent about ninety-eight percent of their time at the firehouse. They were accessible, they were approachable, and they had plenty of time to enthrall us with their tales of great conflagrations and heroic rescues. As far as I was concerned, law enforcement couldn't compare to the thrills and excitement of firefighting.

I do remember that Ruth Ann Phimister's father was a captain in the local police department, but he was never seen except at the school Christmas program when he would appear, to our vast disappointment, clothed in a suit like any other father.

I might mention that Ruth Ann was my first love, but it was

a romance that was doomed from the start. Not only was her father a cop, but her mother was my ninth-grade English teacher. Completely intimidated by two such massive authority figures, I worshipped her from afar, terrified beyond measure even to go to her house.

As for the future, I suppose it was expected that most of us would follow our fathers into their various vocations, a common enough practice, but my father was a printer. Now he was a very successful printer, the owner of his own business, but it wasn't a way of life that set my heart racing at the thought of it.

I mean, how many kids, when asked what they wanted to be when they grew up, would say, "A printer." No, I wanted something more glamorous: I wanted to be a fireman.

There was, however, one incident which occurred during my childhood which may have indicated an aptitude for the law enforcement profession. This was the "Case of the Stolen Baseball Cards," a successful investigation I handled while in the fifth grade. My teacher that year was Mr. O'Ryan, one of my all-time favorites, with a sense of humor I remember to this day.

One afternoon, around 2:30 or so, we were all milling around the classroom, waiting for the bell to ring. With a few minutes left to kill, Chip Brown began showing off his baseball cards.

Chip was a tall, gawky kid with a near-genius I.Q. Although interested in sports, he had been endowed with one of the most unathletic bodies imaginable. Almost totally uncoordinated, he also wore thick horn-rimmed glasses. One final unfortunate touch was that he had been cursed with a tiny button nose for his rather large face, a nose totally inadequate for the job of supporting those heavy glasses. He was constantly pushing them back up on his almost non-existent bridge. This irritating gesture only reinforced his wimpish image.

Since he was hopeless as a ball player, he had to content himself with collecting baseball cards. He had a respectable collection, but one portion of it was unique; he had managed to amass the entire New York Yankees team: every player, every coach, and the team picture. As close as we were to the city, most of us were rabid Yankees fans, but Chip was the only one I knew who had collected the whole team.

As he spread the cards across his desk, we gazed with envy at the priceless collection, and Chip basked in this unaccustomed attention. Even Mr. O'Ryan expressed his admiration.

One person who seemed more envious than the rest was a muscular redhead by the name of Rob Clark. Rob was one of the school's better athletes and also something of a bully. He was Chip's main tormentor, and I could tell he wasn't pleased that the spotlight was on Chip the bean pole for a change.

When the bell rang, Chip left the cards on his desk and went to get his coat. I was standing at the door talking to a classmate, when Rob shoved me out of the way and literally ran down the stairs. I didn't think too much of the incident, since Rob tended to be rather physical when he was in a hurry. There was also the fact he wasn't exactly an admirer of mine. I was as hopeless an athlete as Chip, and Rob had little regard for people like us.

Heading home I stopped at the ball field to watch baseball practice. I stayed for a little while and then, as I turned to go, saw Chip coming slowly down the sidewalk. Head down, he was just shuffling along, not even bothering to push his glasses up although they were teetering on the edge of his nose. He looked as though he could use some company.

I caught up with him. "What's wrong, Chip?"

He glanced at me and said mournfully, "Someone stole my baseball cards when I was getting my coat."

I stopped dead in my tracks, "Not your Yankee cards?"

"Yeah, the whole team."

I felt sick. Who could have committed such a dastardly deed? I walked along in silence with Chip, sharing his misery. I could only imagine how he felt. Those cards were his life. I played the afternoon events back through my mind, trying to come up with some clue. I had seen the cards on the desk when Chip went

10

to get his coat, but I hadn't noticed anything unusual, other than when Rob came barreling through the door, running like the hounds of hell were after him.

Come to think of it, that was about the same time Chip's cards must have been stolen. Surely Rob wouldn't have stolen the cards right off his desk? But what else could explain his strange behavior? "Hey, Chip."

"Yeah?"

"I think I know who might have stolen your cards."

He whirled around, "Who?"

I told him of my suspicions. He agreed it was possible Rob was guilty but pointed out the evidence was essentially circumstantial. We had no real proof, and to accuse Rob of the crime on the basis of such flimsy evidence was risky.

Chip's fears were well-founded. Rob was as good with his fists as he was with ball and bat. He could make ground beef out of both of us in short order if so inclined, and he had a flaming temper to match his red hair. No, it would be suicidal to go off half-cocked. What we needed was hard proof, and that was the problem.

We discussed it for some time, and, after a while, the semblance of a plan began to take shape. I would go to Rob's house and try to catch sight of the purloined cards. I wasn't sure how I would manage this, but, if I could confirm that the cards were in Rob's possession, we would have the proof we needed.

When we were only a few blocks from Rob's house, I told Chip to hide around the corner and wait for me to come back. I almost gave up the whole idea right then when he asked plaintively, "But what if you don't COME back?"

I tried to reassure him (and myself) that I would be back soon.

I walked up to Rob's front door, took a deep breath, and knocked. When Rob jerked the door open at once, I almost wet myself. "What do you want?" he snarled.

I smiled nervously, "Oh, nothing, Rob. I was close by, and I thought I'd stop by and see you." I tried to sound casual, but

I felt like running.

He regarded me suspiciously, "Yeah, well, you've seen me; now beat it." He closed the door.

This wasn't working out at all like I had planned. "I just wanted to tell you that was a neat job you did getting Chip's cards like that," I blurted.

After a long moment, the door opened again. Rob gave me a hard look, but there was a note of uneasiness in his voice. "Whatta ya talking about?"

"You know what I mean; I saw you take the cards when Chip went to get his coat."

Rob's tongue made a quick circuit of his lips. "Yeah, well...he owed me those cards. He never gave me the cards I won from him when we were flipping last week."

Now, we both knew that whatever debt Chip had incurred would never have included his matchless collection of Yankee cards. Chip would have given up his spleen first. However, I wasn't about to argue the point. "Oh, I don't care, Rob. What's yours is yours, right?"

"Right," he said doubtfully. "Say, you're not going to tell anyone about this, are you?"

"No, I'm not going to tell, but I think someone else saw you take the cards, and they told Chip, and Chip is going to tell Mr. O'Ryan."

At this news, I saw a jet of real fear pass over Rob's face. Mr. O'Ryan was quite the straight arrow, a Navy pilot in World War II, very big on honesty, integrity, and other manly virtues. If he found out that one of his students had been stealing in his class, life would become exceedingly unpleasant for the thief.

With a cheery wave, I left a very shaken Rob and hotfooted it back to where Chip was waiting. Exultantly, I told him what I had learned. All he had to do now, I said, was knock on Rob's door, and the chances were good he would be so scared he would return the cards without argument.

Chip refused even to consider the idea.

He was too frightened of Rob to confront him. I yelled and pleaded, and finally, after fifteen minutes of browbeating, Chip gave in. He agreed to try only if I promised to tell his parents how he died.

Fearfully, he tiptoed up to the door and knocked. It worked like a dream. Rob almost passed out when he saw Chip standing there and couldn't give him the cards fast enough. He assured Chip the whole thing had just been a huge joke and hoped there were no hard feelings about it. Chip was so paralyzed with terror he could only nod. He accepted the cards, agreed the joke had really been on him, and got the hell out of there.

So ended my first major case. This was as deep as I got into fighting crime until I became a deputy sheriff some 14 years later.

3

GETTING HIRED

"Northwest Florida Ambulance Service."

"Don Parker, please,"a deep voice said.

"Speaking."

"This is Captain Ambrose at the sheriff's department; I believe you applied for a job with us?"

My heart speeded up. "Yes, I did."

"When would you be free to come in for an interview?"

An INTERVIEW! "Ah . . . I could probably make it as soon as. . . oh . . . how about this afternoon?" I tried not to sound too eager, but it was hopeless.

"Would three o'clock be convenient?"

Hell, yes, that would be convenient. "Yes," I said, in what I hoped was a calm voice, "three will be just fine."

I hung up the phone and sat quite still for long minutes, my head spinning. Everyone I had talked with about the job had assured me it would be months before I could expect to be called for an interview, and here it was not quite six days since I had taken the test.

Actually, I had taken the test as a favor to one of my buddies at the ambulance service where we were both employed. He was eager to go into law enforcement but petrified at the prospect of taking the test. He was one of those unfortunate souls who

14

freezes up when a piece of paper with questions on it is placed in front of him.

I found this quirk a strange one, because Barry was usually a supremely confident individual, the type who breezes through life as though on roller skates, gliding past trouble and confusion with an untroubled air, avoiding disaster by inches, oblivious to the chaos he leaves in his wake. An energetic 22, his boyish good looks and friendly personality helped him cut a wide swath through the female population of Pensacola.

His unruffled manner served him well in his job as an ambulance attendant. Although he had been with the company for more than a year, he evinced no desire to move up to the more prestigious and slightly better-paying job of driver. He seemed content to attend to the patients and leave the driving to us more adventuresome types. I figured he didn't really want the added responsibility.

He came to me pleading for assistance. "Look, Don, you've got to help me with this thing. I get nervous when I have to renew my driver's license."

I shrugged, "I'd like to help you, Barry, but what can I do? I can't take the test for you."

He nodded, "I know that. I'm not asking you to give me the answers or anything, just be in the room with me."

I laughed. "I don't think they allow spectators at a civil service test. How do you propose to get me in?"

"I've got it all figured out. You apply for the job, too."

I stared at him. "Apply for the job of deputy?" He nodded. "But I don't want to BE a deputy".

"I know that," he said patiently. "All I'm asking is that you apply for the job so you can take the test, too. Just having you in the room with me will help a lot."

I was still reluctant. "When is the deadline for the applications?"

"No problem. We've got until four o'clock tomorrow."

"Tommorow? Are you nuts? Have you seen those

15

applications? You have to have birth certificates, school transcripts, military discharge papers, all kinds of stuff. I don't even know where my high school diploma is!'' I was breathing hard.

He dismissed my objections airily. ''It's a piece of cake. We get the application, find the certificates, have a picture made, turn it all in, and we're home free. ''He grinned, ''Nothing to it.''

I could only shake my head. ''You,'' I said, ''are crazy.''

Nevertheless, we zipped down to the county civil service building and got the applications. The clerk who helped us was amused at the idea that we intended to complete everything in 24, but she was cooperative. ''Remember,'' she said, ''everything has to be done properly, or you won't be allowed to take the test.'' On that cheerful note, we headed back to the office to begin the task.

Five minutes into the application, I knew we were doomed. There was no way we were going to complete that thing in the alloted time. The application for the top secret clearance I got in the Navy was easier.

Barry was totally confident. He took the mass of paperwork on calls and, as we careened along the streets with siren screaming, sat calmly in the front seat asking me questions. ''Do you think I should mention I got fired from my paper route?'' he shouted.

I slowed at an intersection, checking for oncoming traffic, then shot through. ''I don't know. How far back do they want you to go?''

He studied the form as I whipped around a large truck. ''Well, it says to list all the jobs you ever had, starting with the present and working backwards.''

Flashing blue lights in the distance signaled the location of the traffic accident we were headed for. I shut the siren off. ''I think you can leave off the stuff about the paper route,'' I said, ''but would you consider giving me a hand with this wreck?''

He glanced at the mangled cars and the crowd of people.

16

"Well, I'm pretty busy right now, but I'll try to work it in."

I spent most of that night and the rest of the next day tracking down the necessary certificates, diplomas, and documents, and completing the voluminous application. At 3:47 P.M. the next afternoon, exhausted and punchy, we turned it all in and stood by nervously while the clerk checked each item off her list. Finally she looked up and smiled. "The test is at nine o'clock Tuesday morning, in the classroom across the hall."

Hollow-eyed with exhaustion, I staggered out to the car and collapsed into the front seat. Barry slapped me on the back. "See, I told you there was nothing to it."

At the stroke of nine on Tuesday morning, we were admitted to the classroom for the test. We were just two of 46 other hopefuls and were seated far away from each other. There had been a remarkable transformation in my friend. The supremely confident Barry I knew so well had been replaced by a pale, sweating creature with eyes that darted nervously and hands that plucked fitfully at his clothing.

The test began, and I found it relatively easy. It seemed to be a general aptitude test, and I went through it quickly. From time to time I glanced at Barry, but what I saw was not encouraging. He was running his left hand distractedly through his hair, over and over. Large sweat stains were spreading beneath both arms and around his collar. I caught his eye once, and he tried to smile, but it was more of a grimace. It was a pitiful sight.

I finished the test within thirty minutes but stayed where I was, intending to provide whatever moral support I could in the time remaining. One by one the other applicants got up and left, until only Barry and I remained.

We had until noon to finish the test, and at 11:56 A.M. Barry put his pencil down and stood up. For long moments he stared at the exam on the desk before him. Suddenly, he snatched it up, handed the paper to the test supervisor, and strode from the room so quickly I had to scramble to catch up with him.

He was heading out the front door when I reached the bottom of the stairs. "Wait a minute, Barry," I puffed. He paused until I was alongside, and we walked in silence to my car. On the way back to the office, Barry stared out the window, humming quietly to himself, beginning to recover from the immense strain he had been under. I parked the car and switched off the engine, unsure of what to say.

He continued to stare out the window, his finger drumming on one leg. Finally, he turned to me, and I saw a man at peace with himself. "Boy," he said, "am I glad that's over with."

"How do you think you did?" I asked guardedly.

He smiled, "Oh, I flunked the hell out of it. I didn't even answer the questions on the last page."

I was horrified. "Why not?"

He shrugged and said simply, "I have trouble with tests."

"Ah, what the hell, you can take it again. You'll probably do better now that you know what's on it."

"Damn right," he said with some of his old flash, "I'll ace that thing the next time."

Of course, Barry flunked, and, of course, I passed. In fact, I was rated number 9 out of the 48 applicants. It was a strange thing. I had initially applied more for Barry's sake than my own, but, as I immersed myself in the process, I started to get interested, even eager.

For one thing, the pay was an amazing $533 per month, a 25 percent raise from my ambulance salary and more money than I had ever earned in my life. At that time, in 1970, at the age of 24, it looked like a fortune. The more I thought about it, the more attractive the job became. The uniform, the authority, the pay, the very nature of the work, it all began to appeal to me more and more.

Now I was going to be interviewed. I had watched enough cop shows on television to figure the interview board would probably consist of a group of senior officers sitting around a table grilling me with tough questions designed to put me under the maximum amount of stress. The more I thought about the interview, the more nervous I became.

One of the city cops stopped by the ambulance service during the morning, and I asked him about his oral interview. He told me he was asked how he would react if he were at a party and one of his friends, knowing full well he was a cop, pulled out a joint and offered it to him.

"What was your answer?"

He laughed. "I hemmed and hawed for about five minutes and finally said I would refuse it and leave the party."

"Did they accept that?"

"I guess so; they hired me."

Later that day, I found another cop who had been asked the same question.

"I told them I would arrest the guy on the spot," he said.

"Did they like the answer?"

"Must have. I went to work a month later."

My head was swimming. Both men were asked the same question, both gave different answers, but both were hired. Of course, they worked for the police department. There was no way of telling what kind of questions they would use at the sheriff's department.

At 2:45 I walked into Captain Ambrose's office looking and feeling nervous. "I'm Don Parker," I told his secretary. "Captain Ambrose told me to be here at three for an interview."

She gave me a warm smile, "Just take a seat. Captain Ambrose will see you in a moment; he's with someone right now."

I sat. The name plate on her desk read "Frances Little." I tried to think of something impressive to tell her, but I was too nervous. The door to the captain's office was open, and I could hear the conversation. I recognized his deep voice, and I heard the thin, whining voice of an elderly woman explaining to Captain Ambrose that her son was "basically a good boy" and got in trouble with the law because he "drinks a little" and how she was one of the few people in the world who understood him.

19

She was trying, successfully as it turned out, to convince Captain Ambrose that she should be allowed to sign her son's bond and get him out of jail.

After 20 minutes of conversation, there emerged from the office a bent, white-haired lady, leaning on a cane, assisted by Captain Ambrose.

We all tend to form mental pictures of people from the sound of their voices, and those pictures are often completely different from their actual appearance. From his voice, I imagined Captain Ambrose to be a fiftyish, heavyset man with piercing eyes and thinning hair. Amazingly enough, he was almost exactly as I had pictured him, except he had only a fringe of hair around a bare scalp. He was just about as bald as I was, and I hoped this gave us some slender thread of commonality.

"God bless you, Mr. Ambrose," she said, touching his arm.

She shuffled out the door, and he turned to me. "Mr. Parker?"

I stood up. "Yes, sir."

"Come in, please." I followed him into his office. He seated himself behind a large desk and began reading what I presumed was my application.

I sat silently, looking around his office. From the various plaques, certificates, and paper-weights, I saw he was a graduate of the FBI National Academy, that he had been recognized as Officer of the Year for 1949, and that he was a member of the Kiwanis.

He continued to read while I thought about the questions I might be asked. There were endless possibilities, but for some reason, all I could think of was the "marijuana at the party" question. I had already resolved to take a hard line and recommend the arrest of anyone who so much as glanced at the pot.

He finally looked up. I decided to try for a little humor to reduce my incredible nervousness. "Well," I said in what I hoped was a jovial tone, "I see we both go to the same barber."

He froze me with a steady, humorless gaze, and my ingratiating

20

smile wilted. "Is that so? Who do you go to?"

I could feel my eyes bugging out. He hadn't caught it at all. I tried to think of the name of a barber, any barber, but my brain was totally locked up in panic. Sweat drops jumped out on my upper lip, and I tried to say something. Finally, I croaked, "Actually, my wife cuts my hair."

He stared at me, obviously puzzled, as I slowly melted into a little puddle and dripped off the chair, disappearing forever into the carpet. He looked down at the folder again. "What kind of training do you have as an ambulance driver?"

His voice penetrated my fog of humiliation and embarrassment, and I snapped back to reality. "Oh, a lot of first aid, extracting injured people from wrecked cars, operating oxygen and resuscitation equipment, that sort of thing."

"Do you know the radio and dispatch codes we use?"

"Oh, yes, sir. We use the same codes as the sheriff's office."

"Fine. Then you could function as a communications dispatcher?"

I nodded vigorously. "I'm sure I could, with a little training."

He made some notes, and I wondered when we would get to the oral interview itself. Obviously, it wasn't going to be held in his office, since it was too small. I assumed we would be going to a conference room somewhere. I kept thinking about the marijuana question and wondered if I should tell the board I would shoot the first person who offered me pot.

Ambrose asked me additional questions about my background, and finally said, "How much notice would you have to give at the ambulance service?"

I thought a minute. "I think a week would be sufficient."

He looked at his calendar, "That means you could start on the. . . tenth."

"I guess so."

He stood up and extended his hand. I scrambled to my feet and shook hands with him. "We'll see you on the tenth then. Report to Sergeant Greathouse in the radio room."

I was mystified. This seemed to be the end of the interview. But what above the oral board, the tough questions? Maybe this was only a ploy designed to see how I would react if I thought I had the job sewed up. He was moving toward the door, obviously ushering me out, and I went, my mind in turmoil. "If anyone ever offers me marijuana, I'll arrest him," I blurted.

He blinked, "How's that again?"

"At a party," I babbled, "If someone ever offers me marijuana at a party, I'll put him in jail."

He stared at me for long seconds and finally said, "Good." He turned away, and I staggered out, writhing in embarrassment but also elated. I had been hired. I was going to be a deputy sheriff.

4

A LITTLE BACKGROUND

Escambia County is located in the extreme northwest corner of the Florida Panhandle. Alabama borders it on the west and north, the Gulf of Mexico to the south, and Santa Rosa County to the east. The county is about fifty miles long and, interestingly enough, the Alabama county directly to the north is also named "Escambia County," which causes some confusion from time to time.

This part of the state does not have the towering palm trees and miles of citrus groves common to south Florida. Most of the trees consist of several varieties of pine and oak. Mostly pine trees. Lots and lots of pine trees.

Although home to some of the world's most stunning beaches, the land away from the coast has a monotonous quality broken only by the abundant rivers and swamps. There are even some hills in this part of the state, an uncommon feature in the table-top flatness of the southern part of the state.

We also have definite seasons in northwest Florida. Admittedly, our six-month summer is bordered by a brief spring and fall, but the three months of winter can be quite chilly, and it is fully possible to freeze to death. The all-time low in Pensacola was five degrees above zero.

While it has its shortcomings, it is still a wonderful place to live. The neon glitziness of south Florida is found only in occasional patches, and big-city traffic jams do not exist, unless you are going to the beach on a warm weekend.

Pensacola, the largest city and the county seat, has a population of approximately 60,000, while an additional 200,000 or so citizens inhabit the rest of the county. The small town of Century is located directly on the state line to the north. With a population of about 2,500, Century is the only other incorporated entity in Escambia County. They even have a small but hard-working police force who, assisted by our sheriff's department, supply the necessary law enforcement.

The law enforcement profession has experienced great changes in the years I have been a part of it. In my early days, college campuses were still in turmoil, cities were still burning, and the Vietnam War still bitterly divided the country. Law enforcement agencies were hard-pressed to deal with the large-scale civil unrest. The low pay and inadequate training did not attract high-caliber people, and it was only the bigger cities which could boast of truly professional police forces.

But I was too naive and too inexperienced to realize how bad things really were. Comforted by the ignorance of my idealism, I was sure I could single-handedly turn things around. Furthermore, I could see no reason why I shouldn't also achieve great fame as an outstanding deputy sheriff, winning a slew of national and international awards along the way.

Ah, the sweet dreams of youth. While I have had a more than satisfactory career, I certainly have not won any international awards. I was named "Deputy of the Month" by a civic club one time, but it wasn't for anything spectacular. I had been doing a lot of crime prevention programs and managed to get my picture in the paper. Someone mistook this publicity for effectiveness and recommended me.

They gave me a really nice certificate but got my middle initial wrong. It came out "Donald E. Parker" instead of "Donald D. Parker". I didn't mind. It taught me a valuable lesson: It was possible to receive recognition for simply doing a lot of talking. It was a lesson I never forgot.

5

THE UNLOADED GUN

As the newest rookie in the communications division, I was assigned to work under the supervision of two other deputies. Both were old salts with 6 months' experience, and I regarded them with awe. Already in rookie school, they were allowed to carry guns. I didn't even have a uniform yet.

I had no trouble learning my job, because all the radio codes were familiar to me from my experience as an ambulance driver. The specific procedures of the sheriff's department, however, seemed amazingly complex. There were individual reports for just about everything and a general type of form for whatever didn't fit any particular category.

I was a bright-eyed, idealistic 24 year-old, determined to be the best cop in the history of the county. I regarded the time I spent in the radio room as a necessary evil to be endured until I would be transferred to the patrol division. The two veterans I was working with were glad to see me and the other three rookies hired, because it meant they were that much closer to being transferred themselves.

They spent a lot of time discussing the merits of individual supervisors and cultivating the deputies on the shift they wanted to join, in hopes they would put in a good word for them with their bosses.

They also spent a good portion of their time studying for rookie school and rewriting their notebooks. They were in the firearms portion of the training now and spent endless hours dry-firing their revolvers, cleaning their revolvers or talking about their revolvers. I hung on every word, longing for the day when I, too, could strap the heavy iron on my hip and walk with that certain swagger that all veterans seemed to have.

The three of us were working a 3-11 P.M. shift and it had been a relatively slow night. With everything going smoothly, one of my mentors decided it was time to clean his gun. Again. I watched with secret envy as he unloaded it, lovingly placing each bullet carefully on the desk. At this point he ran into a problem. He discovered he had left his cleaning kit in his car. He would have to go out to the parking lot and get it.

The moment he left, I casually sauntered over to the unloaded revolver, picked it up, and sighted down the barrel, imagining several bank robbers cowering in terror when they realized the dreaded "Deputy Don" was on the other end. I saw myself ordering them against the wall. One suddenly pulled a gun from his belt, whirled around and . . . the phone rang. Reluctantly, I put the gun down and went to the outer office to answer it.

The owner of the gun returned a few moments later. Before he started to clean the weapon, he picked it up and aimed it out the window. With the phone cradled on my shoulder, I could see him clearly.

There was a faint smile on his face as he cocked the hammer, and I'll bet he was doing a little imagining of his own. His form was perfect as he slowly squeeeeezed the trigger. There was a tremendous explosion, and the gun bucked in his hand. I have never before or since seen an expression of such monumental shock and surprise on a person's face as I did on his. I'm sure it matched the expression on mine. All three of us stared in disbelief at the gun in his shaking hand, a wisp of smoke curling from the muzzle.

It seemed that after I put the gun down to answer the phone, the deputy on the radio took it. When he finished playing, he reloaded it and left it on the counter. Busy with the radio when our buddy came back, he never saw him pick it up.

The bullet somehow missed the glass and buried itself in the heavy steel window frame. A half inch to the right and it would have gone through the glass and into the busy parking lot, with all sorts of gruesome consequences possible.

The owner of the gun and I were running around whimpering and moaning, trying to fan the powder smoke out of the air, convinced we would probably be arrested as well as fired. After all, shooting a gun inside the office, even accidentally, was a serious matter.

Luckily, the deputy doing the dispatching kept his cool. He found some window putty and filled in the hole made by the bullet. There had been some painting going on, and when the putty dried, he dabbed a little brown paint over it. The result was an almost-invisible repair. We were lucky it happened late at night. I doubt if we could have covered it up so well had the offices been full of secretaries and supervisors.

Somehow we got away with it, but we were so terrified we never breathed a word about the incident for five years.

6

THE STORY OF THE EYE

I yawned. Sometimes these midnight shifts in the radio room could really drag, particularly when it was a quiet night. Because it had been so quiet, I wouldn't have much to tell the various media representatives when they started calling. That was going to disappoint them.

Dealing with the media was one of my least favorite jobs as a communications dispatcher. For one thing, we were not supposed to give out very much information; that was the responsibility of the shift commander. However, like most cops, they were extremely wary of talking to media people. That meant the reporters had no one else they could vent their frustrations on except the dispatchers. Naturally enough, we got caught in the middle.

Yes, it was irritating, but this morning I was actually looking forward to the media calls because I had a little surprise prepared for one of the reporters.

Like most new deputies hired by the Escambia County Sheriff's Department, I was assigned to the communications division as a radio dispatcher. This was an excellent training ground for us eager young rookies, but it wasn't what we had in mind.

We wanted to be out in the streets, capturing desperadoes and getting our names in the paper, instead of wasting our lives riding a radio console. We had to endure this purgatory until there was an opening in the patrol division. This interval varied, but a year was about average. I served 13 long months in the radio room.

As the most junior rookie, I was assigned the midnight shift, but it wasn't too bad. I'm a night owl, anyway, so staying up all night didn't bother me. After six months, I was pretty well settled into the routine. There was plenty of activity until the bars closed at 2:30 A.M. After that, there was a lull for several hours. Around 4:30 the media calls would start coming in, asking about the night's activities. Most of the media folks were just working a midnight shift like me, and I got along with the majority of them.

The exception was the newspaper reporter who usually called. He was fresh out of journalism school and took himself VERY seriously indeed. He was from the Woodward and Bernstein school of reporting and seemed to think there was a cover-up behind every tree. He was continually probing for the REAL story, and I found his attitude irritating. As a result, I had not been overly cooperative.

However, on this particular morning, I thought I had a story that might interest him. A few minutes past five he called, wanting the news. I told him it had been a quiet night, except for the "eye."

There was a moment of puzzled silence. "Eye?" he said. "What eye?"

"Oh, one of the investigators found an eye on the sidewalk in front of the jail, but there wasn't all that much to it, so if there isn't anything else..."

"Just wait a damn minute, Parker!" He just KNEW he was onto something the sheriff's office was trying to stonewall. "What's this about an eye?"

"Oh, nothing, really. I doubt if you would even be interested."

"I think I might. Tell me about it."

"Well, I guess you do have a right to know."

"You're damn right I've got a right!"

"Okay. One of the investigators found an eye on the sidewalk in front of the jail last night."

He pondered this information a moment, then burst out, "An eye? A real eye? What are you trying to feed me, Parker?"

"Look, you're the one who wanted to hear about it. If you don't want the story, just say so."

"Okay, okay, I'm listening."

"Well, one of the investigators. . ."

"Which investigator?"

"It was Barlow, Dick Barlow. He found the eye as he was coming in the front door."

"Hold on a minute; let me get some paper in the typewriter." The phone clattered on the desk making me wince. "All right, now, how did he find the eye?"

"It was just lying on the sidewalk. In fact, he almost stepped on it."

Clackety-clackety-clackety-clack-clack went the typewriter. "What can you tell me about the eye?"

"It's grey."

"A grey eye," he repeated. Clackety-clackety-clackety. "How do you know it's grey?"

"Because I can see it. It's here on the desk beside me."

"YOU MEAN IT'S RIGHT THERE IN THE RADIO ROOM?"

"Yes, it's been here most of the night."

"How the hell can you be so calm, Parker? Don't you have any feelings, any compassion?"

"Well, it's just an eye."

"Just an eye," he said sarcastically. "I suppose you pick them up every day out there at the sheriff's department?"

"Well, not every day, but if you've seen one eye, you've seen 'em all."

"Boy, I can't believe you cops," he said, obviously repulsed by my callousness. "Let me get your full name." I spelled it out for him as the typewriter clacked away. "Do you have any

31

idea where the eye may have come from? Do you think it may be some sort of warning, like from the underworld?''

This guy had been watching too much television. ''I'd rather not comment until the results of the investigation are released.''

''Parker, I can quote you on everything you've said so far. It might look better if you told me the whole story.''

''You wouldn't quote me, would you?''

He chuckled nastily, ''Just try me!''

I sighed, ''All right, what do you want to know?''

''I want to know about the investigation. What kind of leads do they have?''

''Well, actually, the case is already closed.''

''Already closed? Why the hell didn't you tell me that in the first place?'' The typewriter was clacking frantically. ''Well, what's the story? Where did the eye come from?''

''I guess it fell out of the sign.'' Snap, went the jaws of my trap.

''Fell out of the sign,'' he repeated automatically. Clackety-clackety. . .suddenly the typewriter paused in mid-clack. ''What do you mean, 'fell out of the sign'?''

''The sign in front of the building. I think it was the 'i' in the word jail.''

There was a moment of shocked silence; then he realized what I had done to him.

''You BASTARD!'' he shrieked, and the phone slammed down.

Our relationship went into a sharp decline after that.

7

ALL IN A DAY'S WORK

I worked as a communications dispatcher for thirteen long, boring months, until I was finally transferred. I was a pretty good dispatcher, if I do say so myself, but at that time the job was a lot easier. There was only one radio frequency to deal with (now there are eight), there were only three incoming phone lines (now there are twelve), and there was usually only one dispatcher on duty (now there are as many as ten).

Dispatchers are now civilians, and most are women. They become quite expert at their jobs and are head and shoulders above the dispatchers of my early days. Dispatching is an extremely high-stress job, even more stressful than being a deputy, in my opinion. At least we can take our frustrations out on our customers, roam the wide-open spaces, and take coffee breaks when things are slow. Radio dispatchers are cooped up in the radio room, buried in the windowless basement. They're lucky if they can go to the bathroom.

The qualities that make a good dispatcher are not necessarily the same qualities that make a good deputy. Many deputies are extremely critical of the job performed by dispatchers, and more than a few have made it clear they could do better if given a chance. And they sincerely believe this, too, until they are given a chance.

YOU'RE UNDER ARREST

Laid low by an injury, some deputies have been assigned to the radio room on light duty while they recover. It takes only a few days for them to discover just how tough the job really is. The best dispatchers are able to perform a multitude of tasks at the same time, an ability most deputies lack. I have seen hardened patrol deputies with years of experience reduced to babbling idiots by just one shift in the radio room. Most are thankful to return to the trenches just as soon as they are able.

To get some idea what it's like to be a dispatcher, I have transcribed a short excerpt from an actual tape of phone calls and radio transmissions. While some of the radio signals may be unfamiliar, you should be able to get a sense of what it's like to work in the radio room.

Remember, this is a routine day. No rapes, robberies, murders, or barricaded, hostage-taking gunmen are encountered. It's just one dispatcher of the five on duty, trying to work the radio and handle the phones at the same time.

DISPATCHER: "Communications; may I help you?"

CITIZEN 1:   "Is this the sheriff's department?"

DISPATCHER: "Yes, it is."

CITIZEN 1:   "I need some information."

DISPATCHER: "Yes, sir."

CHANNEL 2:   "45."

DISPATCHER: "Go ahead, 45."

CITIZEN 1:   "Pardon me?"

DISPATCHER: "I'm on the radio."

CHANNEL 2:   "Call my office in the warrant section and see if my 10-12's are there."

CITIZEN 1:   "I CALLED your office."

DISPATCHER: "Sir, that's the radio. Standby, 45."

CITIZEN 1:   "Oh, you're on the radio."

CHANNEL 2:   "Have you called my office yet?"

DISPATCHER: "Stand by unit 45! Sorry to keep you waiting, sir; can you hold?"

CITIZEN 1:   "Yes."

DISPATCHER: "Thanks." (Puts call on hold and dials warrants)

DISPATCHER: "Warrants?"

WARRANTS: "Yes."

DISPATCHER: "45 wants to know if his 10-12's are there."

WARRANTS: "What are 10-12's?"

DISPATCHER: "Visitors."

WARRANTS: "Just a minute."

WARRANTS: (Two minutes later) "What 10-12's is he talking about?"

DISPATCHER: "Unit 45, your office wants to know what 10-12's."

CHANNEL 2:   "Never mind; I'm pulling into the office now."

DISPATCHER: "Warrants, he said never mind."

DISPATCHER: "Sir, are you still there?"

CITIZEN 1:   "Yes."

DISPATCHER: "Do you have an emergency?"

CITIZEN 1:   "No."

DISPATCHER: "My other phone is ringing. Can I put you on hold again?"

CITIZEN 1:   "Okay."

DISPATCHER: "Communications."

CITIZEN 2:   "Yes, someone broke into my house while I was at work and stole all my stuff. I knew this would happen. I called down there three months ago and told you people to do something about those hoodlums who live down the street ..."

DISPATCHER: "Sir . . ."

CITIZEN 2:   ". . . it's a crying shame; a man works hard all his life to get a color TV and . . ."

DISPATCHER: "Sir . . ."

CITIZEN 2:   ". . . gone to work, some hoodlum steals everything he . . ."

DISPATCHER: "SIR!!!! I need some information from you."

CITIZEN 2: "Information? I told you: those hoodlums — what's the matter with you people?!!!"

DISPATCHER: "Sir, I need your name and address so I can send a deputy."

CITIZEN 2: "If you people did your job, I wouldn't need . . ."

DISPATCHER: "Sir, please hold."

DISPATCHER: "Communications."

CITIZEN 3: "Yes, would you tell Sergeant Innis that his beef jerky is in?"

DISPATCHER: "Pardon me?"

CITIZEN 3: "This is Sergeant Innis' office isn't it?"

DISPATCHER: "Ma'am, this is the sheriff's department Communications. Sergeant Innis works the evening shift on patrol."

CITIZEN 3: "Well, he told me to call this number and leave a message when his jerky came in."

DISPATCHER: "Ma'am, I don't know what you're talking about. Is this some kind of code?"

CITIZEN 3: "I'm sorry. This is Louise from Gourmet Foods. Sergeant Innis ordered some beef jerky and said to call when it arrived."

DISPATCHER: "I'll tell him."

CITIZEN 3:   "Would you like to order some? We're running a special on it this week."

DISPATCHER: "No, thanks. I deal with enough jerks as it is."

CITIZEN 3:   "Okay" (Hangs up).

DISPATCHER: "Sir, are you still there?"

CITIZEN 1:   "Yes."

DISPATCHER: "You said your house had been broken into?"

CITIZEN 1:   "No, I needed some information."

DISPATCHER: "I'm sorry. I have another man on hold who had his house broken into."

CITIZEN 1:   "Sorry to hear that."

DISPATCHER: "What type of information did you need?"

CITIZEN 1:   "What's the sheriff's number?"

DISPATCHER: "14."

CITIZEN 1:   "14?"

DISPATCHER: "Oh, you mean his telephone number?"

CITIZEN 1:   "Yes."

ALL IN A DAY'S WORK

DISPATCHER: "436-9510."

CITIZEN 1:   "Thank you."

TWENTY MINUTES LATER

DISPATCHER: "Communications."

SHERIFF: "Is your supervisor there?"

DISPATCHER: "No sir, she just went to the captain's office."

SHERIFF: "This is the sheriff. When she gets back tell her to call me, please."

DISPATCHER: "I'll tell her, sheriff."

LATER

SUPERVISOR: "You were looking for me, sheriff?"

SHERIFF: "Yes. I had another complaint about the radio room. A man called for my telephone number. He was put on hold for fifteen minutes, and even then the dispatcher didn't know my number. If it takes fifteen minutes to give out my telephone number, I'd hate to think how long it would take someone to report their house broken into."

8

WHO WAS THAT GUY?

The life of a rookie can be a bumpy one. Not only is there the constant stress of trying to learn a new job, there is the stigma of being the new kid on the block.

After a month in the radio room, I had adjusted well to the daily routine, but I hardly knew anyone. As I soon discovered, I was not alone.

Larry Shipman had been hired the same day as I, but, since we were both rookies, we were assigned different shifts. One afternoon I was hastily assigned to work the evening shift with him, because several dispatchers had called in sick.

It was late afternoon. I was on the radio and Larry was working the phones, but not much was happening. As usual, we were busy talking about what life would be like when we were finally assigned to the patrol division. In the middle of this conversation, someone came into the outer office. I leaned back in my chair and saw it was the sheriff himself.

Larry turned, "May I help you, sir?" he asked politely.

The sheriff smiled. "No, thanks, just walking around." He picked up the sign-in log.

Now, I knew instantly from the casual way Larry had greeted the sheriff, he had no idea who he was talking to. This was not as strange as it seemed. The fact was we had little chance even to see the sheriff. Our hiring interview had been conducted by the chief deputy. Once assigned to the radio room, we rarely saw daylight, working mostly midnight shifts. The sheriff was strictly a day man who usually stayed at his end of the building.

I wanted to warn Larry but I couldn't think of a smooth way to do it. He was on his own.

The sheriff continued to leaf through the sign-in log, and I could tell Larry was getting irritated. Finally he said, "Those records are not public information."

The sheriff glanced at him, and I think he must have realized this raw recruit had no idea who he was. "Yes," he said, "I know," and turned another page.

This was too much for Larry. "What's your name?" he demanded.

The sheriff finished reading the log, carefully placed it back on the counter, and looked directly at Shipman. "Oh, most folks just call me 'Sheriff.'" With that, he turned and walked out.

Shipman was a statue. He stayed frozen in position, then turned slowly, his face an unusual shade of green. His lips moved, but no sound came out. Finally he whispered, "Who was that?"

I smiled, "Oh, most of us just call him 'Sheriff.'"

9

AT THE STROKE OF TWELVE

"And so," Sergeant Greathouse concluded, "as day shift dispatcher, you'll be responsible for seeing the siren is set off exactly at noon on Saturdays."

"What happens if I forget to set the thing off?" I asked.

He gave me a thin smile. "Let's just say the sheriff would like for that siren to go off every Saturday at noon and whatever the sheriff likes just pleases me plumb to death." The other dispatchers chuckled, and the meeting broke up.

I lingered a while longer to check out the equipment and review the procedures once more. For as long as anyone could remember the strange-looking mechanism had been attached to the wall in the radio room. It consisted of a black box with various wires running from it. On the box was a dialing device, like a phone but slightly larger.

When I asked what it was for, one of the veteran dispatchers told me it was some kind of controller for air raid sirens, but no one could recall its having ever being used. The sirens had been installed around the county during the paranoia of the 1950's, but the system gradually fell into disuse as the fears of being vaporized in a nuclear explosion lessened. We paid little attention to the thing, except to convince gullible rookies it could be used to have a pizza delivered.

A reporter, curious about the huge sirens, made some inquiries. He was assured by county officials the sirens were always ready to warn our citizens of nuclear attack. Why weren't the sirens tested regularly? the reporter asked. There was no need, he was told. Could such a test be arranged? No problem.

So the test was scheduled, but there was a problem. A big one. None of the sirens worked. Embarrassed officials discovered some were completely rusted, others filled with squirrel nests, and some missing altogether. The gleeful reporter wrote a story about the woeful condition of the once-efficient air raid warning system, and all hell broke loose.

Taxpayers demanded something be done, intimating the sirens were all that stood between them and instant immolation from Russian missiles. A committee was appointed to study the problem, and eventually, funds were appropriated to restore the system to its former grandeur.

With the air raid warning system once again operable, sheriff's department dispatchers were given the responsibility of testing the sirens every Saturday at noon. Personally, I regarded it as just another intrusion into our already hectic job. Day shifts on Saturdays were already impossibly busy, especially at noon. The test itself was a relatively simple procedure, just like dialing a phone. A three, digit code was dialed in to activate the sirens. After 30 seconds, another code turned them off. Simple, quick, foolproof.

I was convinced I would screw it up.

The first Saturday went well. I stood poised by the controller and, at noon, dialed in the code. Eyes glued to the sweep second hand of my watch, I waited exactly 30 seconds, then dialed in the shut-off code. It seemed to work okay, but I couldn't tell. We were a half mile from the nearest siren, inside the county jail, surrounded by noisy radios and ringing phones. Short of actually going outside and listening, it was impossible for us to hear the sirens. I needn't have worried.

A few seconds after I shut off the sirens, the phone rang.

"Sheriff's department, Deputy Parker."

"Virgil Stafford here," the voice boomed in my ear. "I heard the air raid siren go off. My watch was 33 seconds fast. What standard do you set your clocks to?"

He had me there. "What do you mean, Mr. Stafford?"

"I mean, what's the base standard for the time checks at the Sheriff's Department? You must have some way to set your clocks accurately."

I looked at my battered Timex. "Base standard?"

"Yes. Like the Naval Observatory. That's what I use. I call Washington. Most accurate time in the world. I'm retired from the Navy myself, so I may be a little prejudiced." His hearty laughter thundered through the phone, and I held the receiver away from my ear.

"Oh, that standard. Of course. That's exactly what we use, Mr. Stafford, Naval Observatory time."

"Well, that's strange. I wonder why my watch was so far off?"

I thought quickly, "I'm sure it's more of a mechanical problem. It takes a few seconds for the sirens to get rolling after we set them off. They're not as young as they used to be."

"By God, neither am I," he shouted, and I jerked the phone away from my ear again. "Be 78 this year, but I'm still going strong, by God!"

"Thanks for calling, Mr. Stafford."

"Keep up the good work, son," he bellowed, and the line went dead.

Jim Meyers, the other dispatcher, was grinning. "Naval Observatory time?"

I shrugged, "No harm done. I'm sure he'll sleep better tonight just knowing how efficient we are."

The next Saturday was a brutal one, and as noon approached we were both engrossed in trying to dispatch a high-speed chase and keep the city police and the highway patrol informed as to the direction of travel. Meyers was on the radio, and I had a phone in each ear. An incoming line lit up, and I put the city on hold to answer it. "Sheriff's office, Deputy Parker."

"Virgil Stafford here," he shouted. "What the hell's wrong with the air raid siren."

I was horrified to see it was six after twelve. I leaped for the dialer. "Are you sure it's not going off?" I said, dialing the numbers.

"Hell, yes, I'm sure. The pole is right next to my house. I've already called the Naval Observatory and . . ." a rising wail drowned out his words. I hung up, waited the 30 seconds, and shut it down.

The chase ended with the suspect's car in the ditch, and things returned to normal. Meyers answered the phone, and I saw him jerk the phone away from his ear. "Just a moment, sir, he's right here. It's Mr. Stafford," he said, extending the receiver.

I grimaced and took it from him. "Yes, Mr. Stafford."

"Virgil Stafford here that siren went off 6 minutes and 42 seconds late."

"Yes, sir. We discovered there were some transformer problems which overloaded the lines in your area and delayed the signal."

"Transformer?" he yelled. "Want me to call Gulf Power?"

"Oh, no," I said hastily, "that won't be necessary. A crew is on the way to take care of it right now."

"Okay, son," he shouted, "keep up the good work."

When I came to work on Tuesday morning after my two days off, I found a note in my box from Sergeant Greathouse which said simply, "See me."

"The sheriff had three people call him at home over the weekend, complaining that the air raid siren was six minutes late," he said. "What happened?"

I sighed. "It's my fault. We got tied up with that chase, and it just slipped my mind."

"Well, try not to let it happen again."

The next Saturday was quiet. We had a new rookie with us, and he was working the phones. I had been thinking about the air raid siren constantly, determined not to forget it again. About 3 minutes to 12, the rookie answered the phone and winced, leaning away from the ear piece. My heart stopped as I heard the boom of Mr. Stafford's unmistakable voice. I vaulted over the desk, slid across the floor, and feverishly dialed in the code; waited, then shut it off.

I wiped the sweat from my face. Throughout this performance the rookie had stood transfixed, mesmerized by my frenetic activity. "This call is for you," he said.

Dreading what was about to occur, I took the phone. "This is Parker, Mr. Stafford."

"Virgil Stafford here," he bellowed. "I called to get a time check from you, and damned if that siren didn't go off 3 minutes and 21 seconds early."

My blood froze. When I heard his voice on the phone, I panicked, naturally assuming our clocks were wrong. "Uh, it's that transformer again, Mr. Stafford."

"The hell you say! Well, I'm calling Gulf Power right now. We depend on those sirens in time of emergency. The least they can do is provide us with good equipment."

"No need to call, Mr. Stafford. I'm sure we can get it straightened out. . ." the line went dead.

Tuesday morning there was another note and another conversation with Sergeant Greathouse. "This time it was 3 minutes early," he said. "The sheriff is concerned. When he's concerned, I'm concerned. Especially when it's one of my men."

I made fulsome promises to do better and swore there would be no further difficulties.

When Saturday arrived, I was ready. I set my watch as accurately as possible, and at 11:55, I was standing beside the dialer. When the second hand indicated it was exactly noon, I turned on the sirens.

Suddenly, there was a piercing scream from the lobby. "Lord Jesus, help us!" I whirled around and saw a short, fat woman, supporting a much taller man, coming through the door. Blood ran in rivulets down his face, soaking his shirt. They staggered a few steps, then he collapsed in a heap.

I hopped over the counter and knelt beside him. He was conscious and breathing well. The woman told me tearfully that he had been defending her honor in a bar fight and ended up the loser, laid low by a pool cue. I propped him against the counter, using my handkerchief to stanch the blood. "I'm sure he'll be fine," I told her. Meyers called for an ambulance, and I stood up.

Several phone lines were blinking, and I picked one up. There was a steady, unearthly howling from the phone. "Hello?" I said. The howling continued. Faintly, in the background, I thought I could hear words. "HELLO!" I shouted, jamming the phone against my ear.

". . . siren. . . can't hear. . ."

It sounded like Mr. Stafford's voice, and was he saying something about a siren? Now what could. . . Oh, my God, the air raid siren! I jumped the counter and raced for the dialer. With shaking fingers I shut it down. I checked my watch. The citizens of the county had been treated to 7 full minutes of air raid warning.

I will not go into the discussion Sergeant Greathouse had with me concerning the incident, other than to say it was not pleasant. According to the sheriff, a goodly portion of his constituents had called, convinced Armageddon was upon them. Additionally, one elderly lady said the shrieking siren had caused her dog to have a stroke.

A week later I was transferred to another shift, and shortly after that, out of communications altogether. I always figured the air raid warning system hastened my departure, and for that, I was grateful. Even now, years later, I never pass one of those big sirens without feeling a certain fondness for them.

10

FIRST CALL

Rookie school was over. I had survived the 13 months in the radio room, I had answered calls and made arrests under the watchful eyes of veteran deputies; now I was ready to try it solo. Tonight would be my very first shift on my own as a deputy sheriff.

As I signed in, I endured with stoic calm the razzing I got from the veterans who were doing their best to embarrass and humiliate me, as all veterans have always done to all rookies. They were in universal agreement that my bloody and broken body would probably be discovered at first light, face down in some stinking alley, done in by a homicidal eight-year-old.

And if, I was assured, I somehow survived this first shift on my own, it was highly probable the citizens of our county would rise up in furious protest when they realized what sort of incompetent excuse for a law enforcement officer had been foisted off on them. When the torch-bearing mob surrounded the jail to express their outrage, the sheriff would doubtless fire me immediately and have my now-disgraced name stricken from the records forever.

I ignored their comments with as much dignity as possible under the circumstances and took my place in the muster room. The sergeant reviewed the day's crimes, then made the district assignments. I was to work the area close by the jail. One of the veterans whispered that this was done so the sergeant could change my diapers when necessary.

We broke from muster and headed for our cruisers, and I couldn't keep a surge of excitement from rising within me. This was it! Although I had spent many hours in it while being trained, my cruiser car suddenly seemed stiff and unfamiliar as I drove it out of the parking lot. Now it was up to me. There would no longer be the comforting presence of an experienced deputy beside me, ready to bail me out of trouble. I took a deep breath. By God, I could handle it! That was the spirit. Full speed ahead, and damn those know-it-all veterans. The jangling feeling of tension began to lessen somewhat, and I felt better.

I reported myself in service, and I got a call immediately. "109, we have a report of a stalled car blocking traffic at the intersection of Highway 98 and Navy Boulevard. Be enroute and assist."

I acknowledged and headed in that direction. I debated whether to use my siren and blue lights. Regretfully, I decided against it, since the policy manual was pretty specific about restricting the use of emergency equipment to true emergencies.

Still, I didn't waste any time getting there, zipping through the traffic as fast as I dared. I arrived at the scene in a few minutes and found an enormous old Cadillac sitting under the traffic light. Scores of cars were backed up. Horns were blaring, tires squealing, and drivers cursing as they tried to edge past the obstructing car in the face of the onrushing traffic.

I made a U-turn and bulled my way into the seething mass until I reached the Cadillac. I switched on the blue lights and lit up the inside of the car with my spotlight. I saw the driver was slumped over the wheel, and my stomach lurched. Maybe he was having a heart attack.

I leaped from my cruiser and sprinted to the car, prepared to save his life. I could almost see the headlines: "ROOKIE DEPUTY SAVES HEART ATTACK VICTIM." I got to the door and received a shock. The guy was immense. He must have weighed 400 pounds. The thought of trying to wrestle him from the car to perform CPR made me cringe. Maybe he was still alive. I reached through the open window and fumbled at his neck, trying desperately to find a pulse in all that flab.

His eyes opened, and he regarded me blearily. "Wassa matter ossifer?" he mumbled. His beery breath washed over me. The guy was drunk!

Although surprised, I recovered quickly. I knew how to handle a drunk, even a 400 pound drunk. "You passed out at the wheel," I said.

He nodded solemnly, "Thass because I'm drunk." His head pitched forward.

"Hey, wait a minute. You can't go to sleep here." I jerked the door open. "You're under arrest, get out of the car."

He opened his eyes, shook his head slowly, and said, "No."

No? Did he say 'no'? Was I going to have to fight on my very first call? His arm moved, and I stepped back quickly, unsnapping my gun. I changed those headlines to read: "ROOKIE DEPUTY GUNNED DOWN ON FIRST CALL." I waited tensely, but he didn't move, so I stepped a little closer. "What do you mean, 'no'?"

"Crippled," he said, pointing to the back seat. I looked and saw a large wheelchair. This discovery completely unnerved me. Nothing in rookie school had prepared me for this. Murderers, rapists, armed robbers, sure, but not a word about how to handle a drunk the size of a rhinoceros, who couldn't walk. I felt like turning in my badge right then and there.

What to do. I fell back on the method used by all confused cops in times of crisis. When in doubt, ask a supervisor. I got the sergeant on the radio and explained the situation as well as I could. He analyzed the problem instantly and growled, "Either put him in jail, or call a taxi and send him home."

A taxi! Of course. Why hadn't I thought of that? That would solve everything. I would get the drunk off the road and also avoid the potentially touchy issue of having to arrest a handicapped person. I had the dispatcher call a cab and, while I was waiting, I set about trying to unsnarl some of the traffic. Through it all the drunk snored peacefully.

In a short time, a green taxi from the Warrington Cab Company appeared. By now I had regained most of my shattered confidence and was ready to take my place as a productive member of society once again. The driver pulled up beside me. "You call for a cab, chief?"

I was in complete control now. "Yeah, can you park beside the Cadillac? I've got a drunk I want you to take home."

He nodded agreeably and did as I directed. We roused the snoring drunk and, after a great deal of effort, managed to lift him into the back seat of the cab. We added the wheelchair, and I drove the Cadillac across the street and left it in the lot of a closed service station.

I had a few bad moments trying to drive the car because of all the hand controls. For a second, I thought I was going to plow into the concrete block wall at the end of the parking lot, but I finally pulled the right lever and the heavy vehicle jerked to a halt about six inches from the wall.

I was drenched with sweat but glad the problem was almost solved. The cabbie and his now-conscious passenger were waiting for me. "I don't believe I know you," the driver said, extending his hand. "I'm Doug Heist."

I took his hand, "Don Parker."

He continued to grip my hand, staring fixedly at me. "You're new, aren't you?"

My discomfort took a quantum leap. It was bad enough to almost screw up my first call, but to have some cab driver realize I was a rookie was almost too much to bear. "I'm, uh, . . new to, . . uh, this district," I finally stammered, trying to imply this was the first time I had worked this particular area.

He was having none of it. "You're new, all right" he said with such assurance that I could feel my ego shriveling. Sweat was pouring down my back; would he EVER let go of my hand? "I heard there was a new guy coming." He finally released my hand, and I snatched it away before he could grab it again. He smiled broadly, "I'll bet this is your first call, too."

I wanted to die on the spot. All I could do was nod miserably, my confidence demolished. He punched me on the arm. "Aw, hell, don't worry about it, you did fine." He lowered his voice, "To tell you the truth, I've been trying to get hired by the sheriff's department myself for eight years."

Great. Just what I needed. A cab-driving cop buff. After wishing me well, he drove off, but not before the drunk tearfully promised to write the Sheriff a letter of praise because I had given him a break. (He never did)

There is a sad footnote to this story. Doug the cab driver was finally hired as a deputy. For the next eight years he was an enthusiastic and hard-working law enforcement officer, intensely proud of his uniform, probably because it had taken so long to earn it. He had a ready smile and a good sense of humor and delighted in elaborate practical jokes, even when he was the victim. We often talked of that first call of mine, and Doug always assured me he had never seen a person more terrified.

Tragically, Doug was shot and killed while trying to arrest an armed hostage-taker, after an attempted bank robbery. He was a friend, and I miss him. His presence at my first call on that hot July night so many years ago is why every detail of it is still as sharp and clear to me as cut glass.

11
FIRST TIME IN THE PAPER

"PARKER!" Sergeant Morgan's bellow cut through the bedlam of the outgoing muster room.

"Sir?"

"Telephone," he shouted. "Take it in my office."

I pushed through the milling throng of deputies in various states of dishevelment after a hard shift on a busy Friday night. The good-natured cursing, the loud retelling of the night's activities and the irreverent, obscene suggestions to one another a now-familiar background roar to me.

Although still a rookie, I was really feeling a part of the shift. Over the past five weeks, I had handled a wide variety of cases, ranging from vandalism to armed robberies. Although no murders or rapes had come my way, I was learning my job. Each day added to my hard-won store of law enforcement knowledge, and as I gained experience, I got better.

Tonight was a good example.

A stolen car broadcast came out around 8:00 P.M. I spotted the car about 30 minutes later. I lay back and followed him for a mile or so, hoping some nearby unit could assist. Although several deputies headed toward me, no one was really close, and I was afraid the guy would try to run. Luckily, he got hung up at a red light. I jumped out of my cruiser, ran up to the car and

53

stuck my .38 in his ear. He never saw me coming. Not only did I recover the stolen car, but it turned out the guy was a fugitive from Oklahoma, wanted for embezzlement.

All in all, I thought I had done quite well.

I walked into the sergeant's office. "It's the newspaper wanting to talk with our rookie hero," he said.

I flushed, "What the hell do they want?"

He smiled sardonically, "They probably want to write your life story after that amazing arrest of yours tonight."

"Well," I said reluctantly, "I guess I'll have to talk to them."

Secretly, I was delighted. All of us loved to get our names in the paper, but we didn't like to admit it. Peer group disapproval of reporters is widespread in the law enforcement profession, but I had noticed an interesting fact: When the TV cameras were around, there never seemed to be a lack of deputies willing to be interviewed.

I picked up the phone. "Deputy Parker."

"Hi, this is Mike Coulter from the *News Journal,* and I wanted to ask about the guy from Oklahoma you arrested tonight."

"Sure," I said casually. "What do you want to know?"

He asked his questions, and I provided the answers in my usual loquacious style. When I hung up, I was astounded to see that twenty minutes had gone by.

"Are you sure you didn't leave anything out?" the sergeant asked, with what I felt was unnecessary sarcasm.

"Well, I just wanted to make sure he got all the facts."

He laughed, "I think you left out his shoe size."

I ignored these comments from an obviously insanely jealous man and walked back to the now-deserted muster room to sign out.

My wife was sleeping when I got home, but I crashed around putting my gunbelt away and hanging up my uniform, until I woke her up.

"How was your night?" she asked sleepily.

"It was okay," I said casually. "Had a pretty good arrest."

No response.

"I said I had a pretty good arrest."

"Huh? Oh, . . .ah. . .what kind of arrest?"

"It was a guy from Oklahoma driving a stolen car. He was wanted for embezzlement, too. Took him down all by myself. I had him handcuffed before he even knew what hit him. I'll probably get a commendation."

She yawned, "That's nice, dear."

"Yeah, the newspaper called, too; looks like they are going to do a story on it." I tried not to sound too eager.

Steady, regular breathing greeted this pronouncement. Damn! She was asleep again. This was frustrating in the extreme. I really wanted to tell someone about the article in the paper. I debated calling my mother, but it was after 1:00 A.M., and, unless it involved a death, it was not a good idea. If I awakened her at this time of the morning just to say I might get my name in the paper, there would be a death, all right, mine.

My brother. I would call my brother, Roger. He was a real night person and would doubtless still be awake. I dialed his number. The phone rang and rang. Finally, on the eighth ring, a sleep-muffled voice whispered, "Hello?"

"Roger?"

"Yeah?"

"It's me, Don. Sorry I woke you; I thought you'd still be up."

He coughed and cleared his throat several times. "I wasn't feeling too good, so I went to bed early." He coughed again, "What's up?"

"Oh, nothing, really; I just wanted to give you a call."

Silence. "That's it?" he said, with a perceptible edge.

"Well," I said hastily, "I did have a pretty good arrest tonight."

"Oh, yeah? Who was it?"

"A guy from Oklahoma who stole a car." It sounded pretty weak. "But he also had a warrant for embezzlement."

There was another silence, longer this time. Finally he said,

"Great," in a flat tone.

I tried desperately to think of some way to bring up the newspaper story. Nothing particularly impressive came to mind.

"Don," he said evenly, "did you call me at 1:30 in the morning just to tell me you arrested some bozo for stealing a car?"

"Well the *News Journal* may do a story on it, and I wanted to tell you so you wouldn't miss it in the paper."

"I feel sure I would have recognized my own brother's name," he said with some heat. "I mean, how many deputy sheriffs in Escambia County are named 'Don Parker'?"

I was beginning to regret the whole idea. "Look, I'm sorry I woke you up."

"Oh, don't even think about it," he said. "After all, what are brothers for? I LOVE being awakened in the middle of the night so my cop brother can tell me about his latest arrest. In fact, I may stay up the rest of the night just so I can read the article." His voice rose, "Hey, I know what we can do. Why don't we get dressed and drive to the News Journal and wait for the papers to come out. That way we'll be sure to get one. What do you say?"

"I say, go to hell!" I slammed the phone down and flopped down in my favorite chair. What a crybaby. You do a good job, and no one cares. Your own brother gets mad just because you call him. Your own wife goes to sleep in the middle of a conversation. Well, they would change their tune when the story hit the paper.

I leaned back in the chair and closed my eyes, imagining a three-column story on page one. No doubt the wire services would pick it up, and I would be deluged with calls from reporters all over the country, clamoring for interviews.

I must have dozed off, because the next thing I knew, the pale light of dawn was illuminating the living room. I glanced at my watch. It was almost 5:30 A.M. I got up stiffly, joints creaking in protest. I was stumbling toward the bedroom when energized by a thought. The morning paper was probably here! Excitedly I checked the yard from the window. Yes, there it was. I had it in my hands in a few minutes, and I stood on the damp grass in the chilly morning air, eagerly reading the front page. I was disappointed not to see the story, but they had wasted that space with boring accounts of the recent presidential elections. I turned to the local section. Surely it would be here. Nothing. I shivered and decided I could peruse the paper much better inside.

I spread the paper on the living room floor and went over it inch by inch. I was sure a story as important as mine would have a separate headline. After all, didn't the *News Journal* want to sell the maximum number of papers, and wouldn't the maximum number of papers sell if exciting, fast-paced, dramatic stories like mine were printed?

Apparently not.

After twenty minutes of searching, I found it. It was in the "Police Log," a section devoted to minor law enforcement happenings. There, sandwiched between a report of a theft from a plumbing supply house and a bar fight was my "story." It consisted of five lines.

It identified the guy from Oklahoma, indicated he was being charged with auto theft, and concluded with these words: "Further charges are pending, according to Deputy Dan Packer."

"Dan Packer"? Who the hell was that? I stared at the tiny print, refusing to believe they had spelled my name wrong the first time it had appeared in the paper. "Dan Packer? How could they screw up a simple name like "Don Parker?" It was maddening. Grumbling to myself, I finally went to bed, cursing all members of the fourth estate.

It was the persistent ringing of the phone that finally penetrated my unconsciousness. I pulled the phone into the bed and found the receiver. "Hello?" I croaked.

"Deputy Dan Packer, please."

I swallowed a few times and muttered, "This is Deputy Don

57

YOU'RE UNDER ARREST

Parker.''

"No, I need Dan Packer," the voice said firmly.

I was beginning to wake up a little more. "Look," I said irritably, "this is Don Parker. If you're referring to the newspaper article, that was a mistake."

"This is Harvey Schmedlap from *Time Magazine,* and we want to do a story on Deputy Packer."

There was something awfully familiar about this voice. "What did you say your name was?"

"Harvey Schmedlap," my brother roared, "Great story; when is the movie coming out?"

I cringed.

Muster that night was not pleasant. I had hoped no one would notice the tiny story. This was not to be. "Why, if it isn't Deputy Packer," Sergeant Morgan said as I signed in, "star of stage, screen and television."

I retreated to the muster room. Although the place was full of noisy deputies, no one seemed to take any special notice of me. Maybe I would escape with only minor bruises to my ego. I glanced at the blackboard, and a chill ran through me. There, in huge letters, emblazoned across the board were the words, "WHO IS DAN PACKER?" The muster room rocked with laughter as the unfeeling animals I worked with observed my horror-stricken face.

For weeks thereafter I had to endure being called "Dan Packer." I heard it in the halls, I heard it in the muster room, I heard it from the dispatchers, I even heard it in the bathroom. I had hoped that the first time my name appeared in the paper would be a memorable occasion. It was.

12

THE SOUND OF BULLETS

"Are you Parker?" the pretty waitress asked.

I looked up from my coffee. "Yes, I am."

"You have a call," she said, pointing toward the phone under the cash register.

I walked to the counter of the little coffee shop and picked up the receiver. "Parker."

"Sorry to interrupt your break," the dispatcher said, "but we have a report that the runaway you've been after is with her boyfriend at apartment 214-B in Moreno Courts."

I wrote the number on my hand with my pen. "I'm on my way." I hung up the phone, left a dollar on the counter, and headed for the door.

I had been fighting crime for almost two years before I even came close to being in a shootout. Naturally, when it happened, it was nothing like I imagined it would be.

It started out as a pretty routine call. The kid I was looking for was a 16 year-old female, missing for a week. I had taken the original report, and the girl's mother was convinced her daughter was with her sailor boyfriend, determined to get married.

The sailor had been AWOL for two weeks and was eagerly sought by the Navy. The shore patrol almost nabbed the swabbie at a local motel, but he went out the back window. Since then, we had all been playing hide-and-seek with the two young lovers, but, so far, their hiding was much better than our seeking.

At least I had an apartment number to check out. With any luck, I might be able to get my hands on someone. Ideally, I should have had someone to cover the back door, but everyone else was busy, so I was on my own.

It was almost dark when I turned into Moreno Courts. Constructed as military housing during World War II, the courts were a series of single-story apartment buildings with four apartments per unit. Now they were low-income housing with rents tied to the income of the renters.

I moved slowly down the street checking the numbers, the sight of my green and white cruiser turning groups of shrieking children into open-mouthed statues.

I was only a few buildings from the correct number when I saw my elusive quarry. About seventy-five yards ahead of me, a couple had stepped from between the buildings. From the glow of a street light, I could make out a scraggly haired guy, wearing jeans and a stained T-shirt. He had his arm around a young girl with long brown hair. My runaway had long brown hair. I was sure it was them.

The fact they were out in the open was not good. It was going to be a little tough to sneak up on them in my gaudy cruiser, but I was going to give it a try. So far they hadn't seen me and were still strolling along, arm in arm. Then I made a tactical error.

In my eagerness, I touched the gas pedal just a bit too firmly. The 386-cubic-inch, four-barrel-carbed engine responded instantly to my prodding. With a throaty rumble, we surged ahead. The scraggly head snapped up, and he spotted me. He shoved the girl back toward the apartments, then did something exceedingly strange.

I had expected him to set a new land speed record for the hundred yard dash. Instead, he turned, fumbled in his pocket for a second, then pointed at me with his arms extended and his hands clasped. I saw the glint of something metallic, then there was a blossom of flame and a sharp pop.

Things shifted to slow motion, because I suddenly realized what was happening. THIS. . .GUY. . .WAS. . .SHOOTING . . . AT. . .ME!!!

There was another flash-pop, but this time I distinctly heard the "z-z-z-z-z-z," of the passing bullet. I was so stunned I didn't even flinch. My assailant wheeled and sprinted for the shadows.

I finally snapped out of my trance, jammed on the brakes, grabbed the microphone, drew my gun, and tried to jump out of the car. My radio transmission was not exactly a shining example of grace under pressure. The first inkling anyone had that I was in trouble was my frantic yell, "THISGUYISSHOOTINGATME!" I didn't bother with such boring details as my unit number, my location, or even if I had been hit.

My car slid to a stop, and I jumped out, gun in hand. Behind me, the radio was going absolutely nuts as everyone tried to talk at the same time. When I finally got to the edge of the apartment complex, my would-be assassin was long gone. He had leaped the fence behind the buildings, crossed the busy highway, and disappeared into a patch of woods. To this day I have no idea if the Navy or anyone else ever captured him.

I did manage to apprehend the girl, however. Sobbing quietly, she was standing where she had been when the shooting started. I placed her in the cage of my car and got on the radio, trying to restore a semblance of order before my sergeant had a stroke.

While I wasn't too thrilled with the way I had handled the situation, at least I hadn't disgraced myself. I was also interested to discover that I had not felt the slightest bit of fear during the shooting. The prospect of having to face my apoplectic sergeant, however, filled me with dread.

13

TRAFFIC STOP #1

"May I see your license, please?"

The pudgy face, stubbled with several days' accumulation of greasy beard, stared at me through the open window; the small eyes radiating hostility.

"May I see your license, please?" I said again, louder this time.

He stared at me a moment longer, then, oh, so slowly, reached for his back pocket. This little gesture of contempt was spoiled somewhat because his spongy buttocks made it impossible for him to extract his wallet gracefully. He finally had to slide forward, grunting with the effort, and twist to one side to free it. He handed the wallet to me.

I handed it right back. "Please take the license out of the wallet."

"Jesus!" he snorted derisively. He withdrew the license with an irritated snap and extended his arm, not even bothering to look at me.

It was a familiar scene to me. The hostile citizen, angry at being caught and taking his anger out on the cop who pulled him over. In this case I had clocked my fat friend doing 63 in a 45 mile-per-hour zone. I opened my ticket book and walked to the rear of his car to copy the tag number.

This guy had made a fundamental mistake. It was not the fact he was speeding; after all, everyone speeds at one time or another. No, his error was his attitude.

If he had displayed a more pleasing attitude, there was an excellent chance I would have let him go with just a warning, because I don't like writing tickets very much. Oh, I wrote enough to keep the sergeant off my back; but, generally, I tended to be pretty easy on routine traffic violators.

Unless they made me mad.

I completed the citation and walked back to his window. "Mr. Bates," I said, reading his name from the ticket, "I have written you a citation for going 63 in a 45 mile-per-hour zone. If you want to plead guilty, you can mail the fine to the address on the bottom of the ticket."

Bates yawned theatrically, his face a study in bored contempt. In spite of myself, I could feel the old temper start to rise. Usually I will take a certain amount of abuse in stride, but this guy was starting to get to me.

I continued, "If you want to contest the charge, you will have to appear in traffic court." I extended the citation book and a pen, "Sign on the line where I've marked the 'X' please."

"What happens if I don't sign?" he asked belligerently.

I was ready for that one. "Then I'll have to take you to jail."

"Take me to jail?" he yelped. "What the hell for?"

"So you can post a bond," I said with fast-ebbing patience. "If you sign the ticket, it only means you are promising to appear in court, not that you agree with the charges."

I willed him not to sign, but something in my expression must have tipped him off. He glared at me, then grudgingly accepted the pen and scrawled his name. I took the citation book from him and began separating the copies from the carbons.

He got a little braver, now that the confrontation was almost over. "I guess you think you're pretty hot stuff," he sneered, "stopping people for speeding. Doesn't it get in the way of your coffee breaks?"

I had to give him credit for that one. It was pretty good.

I handed him his copy of the citation. He took it between his thumb and index finger as though it were a soiled tissue. "I would think a big, bad cop like you would have better things to do than write people tickets."

This guy was a real sweetheart, and my life was becoming more enriched the longer I stayed in his presence.

I turned and started toward my car. His voice followed me. "Why the hell don't you spend some time catching criminals," he said loudly. "Why don't you catch the scum who cause the real problems?"

I looked back, "I just did."

There was an instant of shocked silence, followed by a sputtering sound as he found his voice. "You bastard, I'll call the sheriff about you. You can't...."

Further conversation was terminated as I closed the door to my cruiser.

An hour later, the sergeant called me into the office. "Did you write a speeding ticket to someone named, 'Bates'?" he asked.

"Yeah, he was doing 63 in a 45." I sighed, "I figured he'd make a complaint."

"Well, you figured right." He shook his head. "He was so mad, I thought he was going to come through the phone. He says you called him scum. Did you?"

"Not exactly, but I sure wanted to."

He grunted, "Yeah, so did I."

I related what had occurred. When I finished, he said, "In the future, don't be so quick to stick people with that wit of yours. He wanted me to call the Sheriff about you."

I waited.

"I declined," he said in reply to my unasked question.

"Well, I appreciate that."

He waved me out of the office. "Forget it. I expect the boss would have given him an earful of good advice about what he could do with his complaint.''

I walked back to my car, reflecting that it was nice to be in a business where the customer is always wrong.

14

HOW TO INTERROGATE
A SUSPECT

My heart sank when I saw the man waving at me from the side of the road. Damn! That probably meant another car burglary, the fourth this morning. I pulled in behind the big Pontiac with the Wisconsin plates and stepped from my cruiser.

He was a portly gentleman with thinning, windblown grey hair. His loud print shirt, Bermuda shorts, black socks, sandals and vivid red sunburn the standard uniform of a tourist. In this case, a very unhappy tourist.

The glass from the shattered door window sparkled in the sunlight. Glass was on the ground beside the car, on the front seat, even on the dashboard. Whoever had smashed the window had used enough force to fell an oak.

"I was just down on the beach," he said in the nasal tone of a Midwesterner. "I wasn't gone 15 minutes. I come back and find this." He looked in disbelief at the destruction. "Got my camera and my billfold." He shook his head, "I can't believe it."

I sighed, "It doesn't take long, I'm afraid."

"But I was only gone a few minutes."

I took the necessary information for the report and spent some time dusting the car for prints. Sweat dripped steadily down my face as I worked under the blazing sun, and my mood was not improved by the several dozen curious beach goers who gathered to watch me work.

They all asked the same question, "Someone break into the car?" I grunted "yeah" to the first dozen or so, then remained mute.

When my continuous silence greeted the inquiries of the new arrivals, they turned to each other. "Someone break into the car?"

"I think so, but I just got here."

"Looks like they broke a window."

"Yeah, I think they did."

"What did they steal?"

"I don't know, I just got here."

"Someone break into the car?"

And so on.

I finished dusting the car and wiped the black powder from my hands. I had found no usable prints.

The owner had been standing by anxiously. "Do you think you can get any of my stuff back?"

"Well, it's certainly possible," I said, trying to sound optimistic. "After all, we do catch these guys." We caught them all right, about one out of every 50, but I assured him I planned to make it my life's work to bring this particular criminal to justice. I wrote down the name of his hotel and got back in my car.

Car burglaries have been, and always will be, a problem on the beach. Innocent tourists, intoxicated by the astounding beauty of northwest Florida's sugar, white sands and turquoise waters, flock to our beaches in huge numbers. Trusting souls, they carefully lock their valuables in their cars and head for the water.

Many do not realize that greedy eyes have watched their departure with interest. When they are safely out of sight, an expertly used coat hanger, a professional unlocking device like a "Slim Jim," or simply a tire tool applied briskly to a window, allows quick access to the car. In seconds the purses, wallets and watches, carefully "hidden" under the seat, are gone.

YOU'RE UNDER ARREST

Cash, credit cards, and jewelry are usually kept and the purses and wallets discarded. Frequently, the entire haul is concealed for later retrieval.

Interestingly enough, window smashers are among the most difficult of the car burglars to catch. Even with their rather dramatic method of entry, they rarely attract attention, but, even if they do, there aren't many phones on the beach. They are in and out in seconds and hardly ever leave any detectable fingerprints. They're a real pain.

I worked my way down the highway, which was jammed with vehicles and people. Both sides of the road were solid lines of parked cars. I could only creep along, dodging barefoot kids high-stepping across the hot asphalt. The road was as straight as a string here, and in spite of the flocking humanity, I could see a long distance. And I knew exactly what I was looking for: I was looking for someone looking for me.

Most I ignored: the heads that turned in surprise as my marked cruiser car passed, wisecracking, teenage studs trying to impress their gum-chewing girl friends, the little kids who waved timidly. No, I was looking for the silhouette of someone scanning the horizon for an approaching cruiser car.

Ten minutes later I saw him.

He came into view along a stretch of sand dunes that had been empty a moment before. He spotted me at the same instant and disappeared from sight, but not before I got a glimpse of shaggy dark hair, a bright blue shirt, and red cut-off shorts. I speeded up as much as I dared, weaving through the throngs of beach people. I was trying to guess what he would do. If he was a pro, he would take off his shirt and hit the water. I'd never spot him in the wall-to-wall crowds.

I squeezed into a vacated parking place, angering a taxpayer in the other lane who had been waiting patiently for the traffic to break so he could take it. I ignored the dirty look and trotted into the sand dunes, drawing stares from the curious sun worshippers. Slogging through the ankle-deep sand in street shoes was hard work, and I was quickly soaked with sweat. Puffing hard, I made a quick circuit of the beach but didn't see anyone who resembled my quarry. I wiped the cascading perspiration off my face and headed back into the dunes.

He was right where I thought he would be, crouching in a little depression with his back to me, watching my car. "Looking for someone?" I asked.

He spun around, but I had him firmly by one arm and snapped the cuffs on him immediately. I wasn't about to try and chase some teenager in this heat.

The shock of my sudden appearance and the quick application of the handcuffs had left him speechless for a few seconds, but he found his voice quickly enough as we started toward my car, sliding down the steep dune. "What are you grabbing me for?" he said, "I ain't done nothing."

"I think you know why," I said ominously, hoping I'd intimidate him. It was a wasted effort.

"I ain't done nothing," he repeated.

I stood him against the cruiser and patted him down. He had only a pack of cigarettes, a disposable butane lighter and a billfold. The billfold interested me because it was stuffed with cash. There must have been over $200. Loot from his break-ins, no doubt.

"You earn this mowing lawns?"

He didn't reply.

His identification showed he was 18, which was a break since I could book him as an adult, if I could book him at all. Right now, I didn't have much of a case.

I gave him his Miranda rights and told him he was under arrest for breaking into cars. I placed him in the back seat, and we headed for the office.

He kept up a steady stream of whining all the way, bitching that I had no right to hold him, complaining that the handcuffs were too tight, demanding to know where we were going.

"Look," I said, "you've been breaking into cars. You know

it, and I know it, so why not make it easier on yourself. Tell me where the stuff is that you stole, and I'll give it back to the owners. Maybe they won't press charges." They might not, but I sure as hell would, since this was a felony.

"I don't know nothing about breaking into no cars," he muttered, but he looked very uneasy. This was no hardened criminal. He was a scared kid, which meant it should be easier to get him to confess, and I badly needed a confession. At this point all I had was an eighteen-year-old with a wad of money. Not exactly conclusive proof. Still, I was sure I had the right guy.

I was relieved to see the sergeant's car outside the substation. I put the kid in a cell and walked into the office.

Sergeant Lewis A. Davis was leaning back in his chair, looking out the window, wreathed by the smoke from his ever-present cigar. He was a lean, slow-talking, slow-moving man. I always thought he would have made a great cowboy. He had enormous patience and displayed a simple, country-boy manner that many people underestimated. His ability to extract valuable information from nervous witnesses and confessions from uncooperative arrestees never ceased to amaze me.

He nodded as I came in. "Bring us some business, Donald?"

"I hope so," I said. "I think I've got the guy who has been popping the cars down the road." I explained the circumstances of the arrest, admitted I had very little to go on, and said I was probably violating most of his constitutional rights by detaining him with no proof. Louie raised an eyebrow at this, and I concluded hurriedly, "But I'm sure it's him, Sarge. He's got a pocket full of cash, he was in the general area, and he acted right." I sighed, "I just can't prove it."

He studied the end of his cigar for a long moment, then said, "Well, I guess you've got a problem, then."

I flushed. "Well. . .I was hoping you might talk to the kid, maybe bluff him. . .or. . .something."

He smiled, "It's hard to run a bluff if you don't have any cards."

70

I nodded.

Another long moment of silence passed. "Well, bring him in. We can at least talk to him." I fetched the kid from the cell and seated him in a chair in front of the desk. The kid immediately launched into a long, rambling dissertation concerning his total innocence, the severe retribution he was going to exact from the department when he sued, his general unhappiness with the situation in general and me in particular.

Louie listened quietly, puffing now and then on the stogie, asking occasional questions. Finally he asked the kid if he had been around any of the cars that had been burglarized.

"No, sir!" the kid said emphatically. "I ain't touched them cars."

Louie nodded agreeably and opened a side drawer in the desk. He rummaged around and withdrew a white card. I recognized it immediately. It had old fingerprints on it, lifted from some long-ago burglary. These particular prints were sharp and clear, a real textbook illustration of what latent prints should look like. Too bad we had never been able to match them up with a suspect. The card had been in the desk for at least a year.

"You say you've never touched any of those cars?" Louie asked again.

"No, Sir!"

Louie stared at him a moment longer, then casually spun the fingerprint card toward him. The kid grabbed it reflexively. "Then, how do you explain that?" Louie said.

As the kid looked at the ancient prints, the blood drained out of his face. His hands started to tremble, and suddenly he began to cry. "All right, I did it," he bawled. "Please don't put me in jail, mister."

Louie pointed at me with his cigar. "You show this deputy where the stuff is that you stole, and we'll talk about it."

The kid and I spent the next hour digging through trash cans, retrieving the items he had hidden. We also recovered the length of pipe he used to smash the car windows. When we were

71

finished, I didn't smell too good, but I had most of the stuff back.

I notified all the owners I could find, including the man from Wisconsin. He was pleased and surprised. "How in the world did you do it?"

"It was no big thing," I said modestly. "You just have to know how to talk to these punks."

15

ROUTINE PATROL

My cruiser car rocked as another blast of frigid wind hit it. Even though I had the heater going wide open, I shivered. The temperature was supposed to be in the low 20's tonight, with wind gusts to 25 miles per hour.

When the wind picked up, the sand blew in clouds off the dunes on the side of the road. It reminded me of a snowstorm, and I didn't care for the illusion. Give me the sauna-like heat of the summer any day. If I wanted snow, I would move to Vermont. I continued down the road, driving carefully.

I suppose there are lonelier places than Pensacola Beach in the winter, but I haven't been to any recently. Spending a midnight shift on the beach in the winter is not a job for someone who gets bored easily. Tonight I had worked half the shift, and nothing had happened. Oh, the radio had been alive with all sorts of exciting things, but they were all occurring in town. An armed robbery, a high-speed chase, and a prisoner who tried to escape had kept the rest of the shift busy and left me mad with envy. I wanted to be out catching bank robbers, apprehending axe murderers, or shooting it out with desperadoes. Instead, I was stuck patrolling the sand dunes while my fellow deputies covered themselves with glory.

My sulking was interrupted by something on the side of the

road. Far ahead I could see the ruby glimmer of taillight reflectors, and my depression lifted slightly. Perhaps this was a car full of drug smugglers preparing to off-load several hundred pounds of cocaine from a boat out in the gulf. Maybe the car held the gruesome remains of some hapless murder victim. My heart began to thump a little faster, and I pulled my coat aside to allow better access to my revolver.

There were no signs of life around the car, and when I got beside the vehicle, I saw the left front tire was flat. There was no way of determining how long the car had been there. I resumed my monotonous patrol, more depressed than ever.

Next I checked the residential areas, house by house, diligently shining my spotlight on possible locations for break-ins. Of course, I found nothing. No burglar in his right mind was going to be out on a night like this.

Hours later, as the sky began to lighten, they finally called my number.

"109?"

I was paralyzed with surprise.

"Headquarters to 109," she repeated.

I grabbed the microphone. "Go ahead, I'm still on the beach." At last. Maybe the night wouldn't be a total loss.

"10-4, 109, what car are you driving?"

"Uh...car number 136." I waited, but there was only silence from the radio. I keyed the microphone again. "Did you read me, headquarters?"

"10-4, 109. Thank you." the radio was silent again.

That was it? Just the number of my cruiser car? I couldn't believe it! It was the only time they called me all night.

16

HOW TO KILL
A RATTLESNAKE

I was lingering over a cup of coffee at Butler's Restaurant on the beach one afternoon when Deputy David Hammond, sounding very worried, called me on the radio.

"109, can you come to Sabine Drive?"

"10-4," I said, "What's the problem?"

"I was flagged down by a resident. They have a rattlesnake in their back yard, and I think I'm going to need some assistance."

A rattlesnake? Visions of an enormous diamond-back with two-inch fangs dripping deadly venom, danced through my head.

"Do you read me, Don?" Hammond asked anxiously.

"10-4," I said quickly, "I'm on my way." I left a tip and went out the door.

Law enforcement is a people job and, as might be expected, people cause most cops their biggest problems.

Most cops. But not me. Animals have always caused me the most trouble. Crawling animals, flying animals, jumping animals, swimming animals, slithering animals: any kind of animal. I have had my moments with people, but if there is going to be a serious problem with the chance of serious embarrassment, some animal will wait until I am the Deputy on duty to cause that problem. Like this rattlesnake.

Butler's was only a mile or so from Hammond's location, and

I arrived within minutes. His cruiser car was parked in the driveway of an expensive home. I was dismayed to see a crowd of adults and children milling around the yard. An audience might make our job, whatever it was going to be, more difficult.

David met me in the driveway. "The snake is behind the house, Don, but I can't get close to him." He wiped the sweat from his face. "Every time I move toward him, he strikes."

God, this was worse than I thought. We walked around the house, followed by a gaggle of chattering children pelting us with questions.

"Are you going to shoot him, mister?"

"Can I have his fangs?"

"Will you skin him for me?"

"Can I cut off his rattles?"

"Don't hurt him, I want him for a pet."

Kids are wonderful.

We reached the back yard, and David pointed toward the edge of the house. "He's there, in that corner," he said in a low voice. I wondered if he thought loud talking might anger the snake.

I looked where he pointed, but at first I didn't see anything as the grass was a bit overgrown. I continued to scan the ground, and finally I saw a movement. A small, triangular head lifted above the grass, then dropped to the ground. I looked more closely and saw the outline of an equally diminutive body. "THAT'S the snake that is causing the problem?"

"Listen," he said with some heat, "that thing is vicious! You try and get close and see what happens."

I studied the little reptile. I was pretty sure it was a pygmy rattler, fairly common on the beach. The term "rattlesnake" when applied to this species is a misnomer since they rarely have an audible rattle, but they are venomous and rather pugnacious, too. This one appeared to be about twelve inches long but didn't look very threatening.

I happened to know that Hammond was deathly afraid of snakes, so I made allowances for his nervousness. I decided to get a little closer.

76

I took a few steps forward, and the little snake coiled up. The wedge-shaped head rose from the grass, the yellowish eyes watching me coldly, the forked tongue darting in and out, testing the air. I had to admit the snake did look unfriendly.

When I was about four feet from him, the reptile suddenly lunged. I doubt if the strike covered more than six inches, but I jumped back. There was a titter from the crowd, and I flushed.

"What'd I tell you," Hammond said smugly.

"Yeah, well, it just caught me by surprise."

He smiled.

It was time to take command here. "All right, everyone move back." The kids retreated about a foot, then surged forward as soon as I turned around. "I think we're going to have to kill it." I told Hammond. This brought a cheer from the bloodthirsty kids. "Let's see what our options are."

Hammond looked at the snake darkly. "I say let's shoot the damn thing." Another cheer.

I studied the terrain. The house was constructed on a concrete slab. Shooting toward the ground would likely guarantee ricochets off the concrete. This could cause some P.R. problems for the department if the ricochets dropped some of the watching children, although I had several in mind. The kids weren't the only concern. Directly above the snake was a large picture window of expensive tinted glass. I didn't think its value would be increased by the addition of bullet holes.

No, shooting was out of the question. I decided we would have to beat it to death, and soon. The snake was getting restless. "We're going to have to get something to hit it with," I said.

Hammond's face lit up. "I've got just the thing," he said excitedly. "Wait here." He ran to his cruiser car, opened the trunk and retrieved something. He trotted back to where I was standing. "Here." He handed me a tapered stick about two feet long.

"What the hell's this?"

"It's a sawed off pool cue I took off a drunk," he said proudly.

It seemed awfully short. "You think we can kill it with this thing?'' I asked doubtfully.

"Oh, yeah, I'm sure you can," Hammond said.

"Me? Why don't you do it?"

"Because you have the pool cue."

"But it's your call."

"That's all right; I don't mind sharing."

I was going to argue further, when one of the little urchins said loudly, "I think he's chicken."

I gritted my teeth. Now it was a question of honor. I gripped the pool cue and advanced. The snake coiled and raised his head, watching me warily.

It was an amazing thing. The closer I got the larger the snake seemed to become. Was it growing? The now massive head swayed back and forth, no doubt searching for a spot to inject a lethal dose of venom. My steps became, slower and I could feel the cold sweat on my face. All my original fears bubbled up within me. The thing looked as big as an anaconda now. The snake suddenly struck. I lashed out with the pool cue and the weapon thudded into the ground.

It was at least a yard short.

Gales of laughter erupted from the kids. Even the snake seemed amused. I could have sworn his malevolent yellow eyes had a certain mocking twinkle to them.

It was a fatal error. It was bad enough the kids were laughing at me, but I couldn't stand to have the snake laughing, too. Enraged and humiliated, I brought the pool cue crashing down on his scaly body. He struck ineffectually at the hard wood, and I hit him again. And again.

347 times.

Hammond said later it sounded like a woodpecker on an oak tree.

When all movement ceased, I stepped back, breathing hard, and raised the pool cue over my head. Waves of cheers from the kids washed over me. They crowded around while I delivered the coup de grace by cutting off its head with my pocket knife. I put the remains in a paper sack, then locked it in the trunk of my car. I wasn't about to dispose of the snake on the premises and have some inquisitive seven-year-old dig it up later.

I went back to the beach office and typed a somewhat humorous account of the incident. I turned it in at the main office later that day and thought no more about it.

The report wended its way through the paperwork pipeline, and one of the clerks in records read it and found it amusing. She showed it to several others who also enjoyed it. Eventually, someone called one of their friends at the paper. The reporter thought it was funny enough to print. Verbatim.

Of course, all this was happening without my knowledge. The first I learned of the story was when my mother woke me the next morning, calling to gush over the article.

After some confusion, I finally figured out she was talking about the rattlesnake and was horrified when she read the story to me over the phone. The department has strict rules about news releases, and I wasn't at all sure the sheriff would be pleased.

As soon as I could, I got off the phone and galloped outside to retrieve the paper. It was just as my mother said. The report was in there, all right, word for word.

When I got to work that afternoon, there were phone messages from several radio and television stations. I returned the calls, and they all wanted more information about the rattlesnake. Several wanted interviews which I flatly refused.

I couldn't understand this fascination with what I regarded as a minor news item. I soon discovered the one thing media folks like almost as much as blood-and-guts stories is human-interest stories, particularly, humorous human interest stories. Like the story about the rattlesnake.

The deputies who worked with me were agog. It was unusual enough to just get your name in the paper, but no one could recall anyone having their entire report printed.

Still nervous about the sheriff's reaction, I tried, with little success, to play down the incident. They weren't having any of this. "Hell, he can't fire you," one of the guys said, "you're famous."

I wasn't so sure. I went to Butler's to have lunch, but the locals swarmed around me so persistently, talking about the article in the paper, I lost my appetite. I was beginning to understand how real celebrities feel when they go out in public.

As luck would have it, a retirement ceremony was planned that afternoon, so I would soon learn how the sheriff felt about the story.

I waited until the last minute to sneak into the room, hoping to be as unobtrusive as possible. As soon as I came in the door, I was spotted by the other deputies. "Look, it's the snake man!" someone shouted, "Did you have to pay for all the publicity?" someone else asked.

Further comments were cut off as the sheriff came in. He walked to the front of the room and stood behind the lectern, arranging some notes. He looked over the crowd, saw me, and grinned. "Well, I see we have the snake killer with us today."

The room exploded with laughter. Actually, the line wasn't that funny, but everyone laughs when the sheriff makes a joke. My cheeks were burning, but I was relieved. At least he wasn't angry.

The kidding continued after the ceremony was over, but now I basked in the attention. Learning I was not in trouble had taken a great weight off me.

That night most of the local stations at least mentioned the story, and calls from friends and relatives poured in. It was nice, but by bed-time I was getting a tad weary of the attention, particularly because the comments were beginning to sound the same.

The next day I went through it all again as people I hadn't seen since the incident had their say, and they all said the same thing. This tedious lack of originality began to get on my nerves, and my smiles were becoming forced.

The scene in Butler's was a repeat of the day before: I could hardly take a sip of coffee without some cretin coming up with something terribly original like, "Hey, Don. Killed any snakes lately?" or, "I got plenty of snakes around my house, how about coming over and killing them for me?'' or, ''Say, Don. Who's your press agent?'' or, ''Is it true you wet yourself when that snake came after you?''

By the end of the day, I was heartily sick of the comments, and I fear I may have been a little short with one or two well-meaning but irritating admirers.

I figured all the excitement would die down within a day or so, but it was still going strong at the end of the week. I could not believe so many people had read the story. Each time I ran into someone I hadn't seen in a while, I suffered again. Eventually things returned to normal, but the snake story still cropped up from time to time.

One night, weeks after the event, I arrested a drunk after a bar fight. As we headed toward the jail, he asked me my name. ''It's Parker, Don Parker,'' I told him, figuring he was going to make a complaint.

He considered this for a time, then said thickly, ''Ain't you the one who killed the rattlesnake?''

My birthday is in September, and one of my in-laws gave me a little rubber snake as a gag gift.

When I was transferred back to the main office after being stationed on the beach for two years, the deputies who worked with me gave me a little rubber snake as a going-away present.

At the departmental Christmas party, seven months after the original incident, I was presented with a little rubber snake.

At a shift party the next spring, I was given, you guessed it, a little rubber snake.

Even now, years after the demise of that pygmy rattler, I STILL have people ask me if I am the Parker who killed the snake on the beach.

I wish I had never seen that damn snake.

17

EVER HAVE ONE OF
THOSE DAYS?

I saw the winking blue lights a long way off. "Wreck", I
thought to myself, and so it was. I threaded my way past the
trooper who was handling the accident, around the two damaged
vehicles, and then I was clear. I was happy for the invisibility
that being off duty brings. Not that I was needed. It didn't appear
anyone was injured, and the trooper obviously had everything
well in hand. I stopped for the red light at the next intersection
and noticed a rather disheveled-looking guy walking rapidly
toward my car. I rolled down the passenger-side window. "Can
you help me?" he asked.

"What's the problem?"

He leaned in the window. "I really need a ride. It's kind of
an emergency." Up close, I could smell the beer on his breath.

"What kind of emergency?"

He gave me a crooked smile. "Well, to tell the truth I was
in that wreck back there, and I've been drinking." He laughed.
"I'm on probation from a drunk-driving charge right now, and
I can't stand another·arrest."

I had to chuckle, "Sure, hop in."

When the light changed, I made a 'U'-turn. He looked
apprehensive as we approached the wreck, then downright
alarmed as I pulled up beside the trooper. "What the hell are

you doing?'' he hissed, sliding down in the seat.

I flipped my badge case open, and the color drained from his face. ''Brother,'' I said, ''this just isn't your day.''

18

PLANE CRASH

Many of us in the law enforcement profession were initially attracted to it by the image of ourselves as heroes. Certainly this was in my mind when I first entertained thoughts of being a cop. I could easily see myself the object of public adulation as a result of some amazing deed of derring-do, surrounded by platoons of dewy-eyed females, all clamoring for my autograph.

However, it didn't take me long to realize that amazing deeds of derring-do usually required equally amazing risks of the derring-doer. Looking into the hero business a little further, I discovered several other alarming facts.

For instance, many of those heroes surrounded by the crowds of admiring females were in wheelchairs or full-body casts. There also seemed to be a disturbingly high number of heroes whose names were now preceded by the words, "The Late..."

After thinking long and hard about it, I came to the conclusion that the best thing I could do was proceed with my career, maintain a low profile, and applaud the efforts of others.

There was a problem, though. I soon found that in the law enforcement profession circumstances often contrive to make heroes out of the participants, even if those participants have no desire to become heroes. As I was to discover, there is such a thing as being in the wrong place at the right time. A good example of this was the plane crash on Pensacola Beach.

It happened on a bright, sunny day in late February. I was finishing a report at the beach office when the dispatcher called my number. I picked up the radio, "Go ahead, I'm in the beach office."

"10-4, 109," he said calmly, "we have an unverified report of a plane crash in the housing area on the east end of the beach. Check it out and let us know something."

A plane crash? On the beach? I was only a few miles from the east end, and I had not heard anything like a plane crashing. I decided it was a false alarm, but I acknowledged the transmission and headed for the door.

Traffic was sparse, so I didn't bother using the blue lights and siren. As I drove, I scanned the skyline. If a plane had gone down, I was sure there would be a towering column of smoke. Nothing. I passed the volunteer fire department. It was as quiet as a mausoleum. Definitely some bad information.

The first indication that all was not well came a few seconds later when Carl Haber, the chief of the fire department, flashed by me in his private car, headed toward the fire station. I was pondering this development as I turned off the main highway. It seemed peaceful enough — no smoke, no fire, no airplane parts. I was almost to the end of the block when I saw that things were not so peaceful, after all.

A distraught woman was standing in front of an expensive beach-front home, waving frantically. It was easy to see why she was distraught: There was an airplane sticking out of her house.

Actually, all I could see was the tail section, but I was pretty sure the rest of the plane was not far. It had been a small blue and white plane and had entered the the roof at an almost-vertical angle.

The woman ran to me. Her clothes were covered with a fine, greyish powder, and her hair was dusted with more of the same. She didn't seem to be hurt, but there was a wild look in her eyes.

"I was making lunch," she said in a panicky tone. She grabbed me by the arm. "There's a man in there. You've got to help him!"

The front door was open, and I could see a mass of wreckage. It was going to be difficult to get in. Footsteps pounded behind me, and I turned. A Naval officer in a khaki uniform was running across the yard. "I'm a flight surgeon," he said, slightly out of breath, "is there anything I can do?"

This was a lucky break. "Yeah, help me get into the house." We started pulling pieces of crumbled sheet-rock, attic insulation, and smashed lumber out of the way. We cleared a narrow passage and wormed our way through. A large piece of the wing extended from the ceiling, and we squeezed around it into what was left of the family room.

The main part of the fuselage was to our right. The cockpit had been split open by the impact, and it reminded me of a beer can I once blew up with a cherry bomb. The ruined instrument panel dangled from the remains, the microphone still neatly clipped in its holder.

The engine had been wrenched from its mounting and rested on, or rather in, a large console television set. Plaster dust still filled the air, and my eyes watered from what I figured was hydraulic fluid or something.

"Over here!" the doctor shouted. There was a body lying face down in the kitchen. We scrambled over the shredded furniture and across the terrazzo floor, splashing through several inches of water, obviously from broken pipes. We bent over the body, which was that of a chunky male, probably in his fifties.

The first thing I noticed was his hair, still intact, lying a few feet from the head. My stomach did a flip. The guy had literally been scalped in the crash. His smooth skull, streaked with blood, gleamed in the dusty light from a shattered window.

While the doctor tended to his patient, I stared with horrified fascination at the soaked scalp there on the floor. The part was still visible, for God's sake! It was so perfect, it could have been a wig. I looked closer. It WAS a wig. The poor devil was bald as an egg, and his rug had not survived the crash.

The doctor was speaking to me, and with an effort, I tore my eyes from the toupee. "He's dead, probably killed instantly," he said.

"We'll have to leave him here for the crime scene photographers," I told him. My eyes were watering so badly I could hardly see, and the fumes from the hydraulic fluid, or whatever it was, made it hard to breath. It was getting to the doc as well. "Let's get out of here," he said, scrubbing at his eyes.

We splashed across the floor and started back over the pile of debris. There was much shouting outside. The fire department had arrived.

We were almost to the front door when I heard a most peculiar sound. It sounded like someone snoring. The doctor was in front of me, crawling over the pile, and I grabbed him by an ankle. "Listen, Doc." He paused. The snoring continued. We looked at each other.

"Someone's in there," he said, pointing to what had probably been the living room. It had taken most of the impact and was jammed, floor to ceiling, with wreckage. We started pulling large chunks out of the way, trying to force a passage into the room.

There was more shouting from outside, then much clattering and crashing as the firemen began to clear a path through the hallway. In a few minutes we were joined by several of them, bulky in their heavy coats and helmets.

"We think someone's in there," I said, pointing. Instantly, they began tearing frenziedly at the debris.

"Don't do that!" the doctor shouted, "One spark and this whole place could go up." They froze, eyes wide. After a moment they resumed their labors in a kind of strained slow motion, pulling pieces loose and placing them carefully on the floor.

With all of us working we soon made an opening. I took off

my gunbelt and slithered into the wreckage. I worked my way past the other wing and began clearing away the sheet-rock and the splintered wood blocking my way.

I was on my belly, facing downward, the sweat running down my glasses and dripping off my nose. The snoring was louder here, and soon I uncovered a badly twisted arm, attached to a body. It was obvious the arm was broken in several places. I worked my way up to the shoulder and uncovered the head.

This was another man, lying on his chest, his breath bubbling and rasping. It took a combined effort to slowly work him out of the wreckage and onto a stretcher. I was the last one out of the house.

I had been so intent on the rescue, I wasn't aware of what was happening outside. As I stepped through the door, blinking in the bright sunlight, I saw scores of people milling around the fire trucks, ambulances, and other emergency vehicles. Dozens of cars belonging to the volunteer firemen were parked at all angles, hastily abandoned by their owners. Spectators crowded forward, trying to get a glimpse of the injured man as he was wheeled toward the waiting ambulance.

As I trudged toward my cruiser, I was grabbed, literally, by a reporter from our local TV station. Wheeling me around to face her camera, she shoved a microphone in my face and asked me if I had been in the plane crash. "No, I'm with the sheriff's department," I told her.

She stared at me, and I began to understand her confusion. My grey shirt was ripped and tattered, stained with oil, blood, and God knew what else. I noticed my badge was missing, probably plucked from my shirt by the wreckage while I was crawling in after the second victim, and my dark green pants were now a mottled greyish color.

In short, I looked very little like a deputy sheriff but very much like a plane crash survivor.

Once we cleared up the identity problem, the interview continued. Many other interviews followed, and at some point,

PLANE CRASH

I recall one reporter or another telling me the man we had pulled from the wreckage had died without regaining consciousness. Finally, it was over. I went back to the beach office, typed my report and went home.

I felt a lot better after a long, hot shower and a thorough scrubbing. As I was drying off, I noticed my feet and ankles were reddened by some sort of rash, but it wasn't uncomfortable, and I didn't think too much about it. Before going to bed, my wife and I watched me on the evening news. I looked and sounded terrible, and it was a relief when the footage ended.

As we were turning off the light, the phone rang. It was the radio room with a long-distance phone number for me to call. In a few moments, I was speaking with an investigator from the National Transportation Safety Board. He would be arriving in the morning to gather the facts about the crash and asked if I could pick him up at the airport. He said he would need my help to locate the various witnesses, and I agreed to do what I could.

He was waiting for me at the front door of the terminal when I arrived. His name has long since flitted from my memory, but he was a stocky man with iron-grey hair, cut in a crew cut. I wasn't surprised to learn he was a retired Air Force pilot. He certainly looked the part. He was smoking a pipe and had a deliberate way of speaking, as though considering each word very carefully. I was very impressed.

On the way to the beach, we talked about the crash. He told me his job was to investigate the crash and gather the facts necessary to determine the cause. He would make his report to the safety board, and they would have the final say.

We spent quite a bit of time in the beach office reviewing my report and discussing what I had seen, both inside and outside the house. After he was satisfied, we drove to the scene, and he took a series of pictures of the sad remains of the airplane, still impaled in the house. After he finished, we went in search of others who might be able to tell us what had happened.

The woman who had been in the house when the plane hit gave

us a vivid account of her experience. She was still very shaky, and when she told of seeing the dead man on the floor of her kitchen, a solitary tear trickled slowly down one cheek.

Nearby residents told us they saw the plane proceeding along the edge of the beach at low altitude. They said the aircraft made a sharp turn and suddenly plunged straight down. Everyone we talked to, including the woman in the house, recalled hearing the engine running until the sound of the impact, so an engine failure was unlikely.

The Navy doctor was last on our list. On the way to his apartment, I told the investigator my theory of the cause of the crash: I figured the two guys had spotted some attractive lass sunbathing in the nude and turned for a closer look. Being low and slow, the plane stalled, and that, as they say, was that. When I concluded my little dissertation, he simply puffed on his pipe, making noncommittal investigator noises.

The doctor lived on the eighth floor of a beachfront condo with a magnificent view of the Gulf of Mexico. He met us at the front door, wearing a bathrobe and looking rather pale. He was barefoot, and I noticed he had a rash on his ankles similar to mine. We sat in the spacious living room while the investigator asked questions and made notes.

As far as I was concerned, I had played a rather insignificant part in the previous day's drama, so it came as no small shock when the good doctor pointed a shaky finger at me and declared, "That's one of the bravest men I have ever seen."

I resisted the impulse to look over each shoulder. "What the hell are you talking about, Doc?"

"I'm talking about the risk we were taking."

The smile on my face disappeared. "What risk?"

"The risk of fire or explosion." He shook his head, "We were damned lucky."

Fire? Explosion? I stared at him as he turned to the investigator. "The entire kitchen was four inches deep in aviation fuel," he said. "We were splashing around in it the whole time."

I tried to speak. "F-F-F-Fuel? You mean, like gasoline?"

"Right." He extended one leg. "What do you think caused this skin irritation?" We all looked at his reddened foot. "I'll bet it got you, too," he said.

I tried to smile. "Well, sure, my feet are a little red, but I thought we were wading around in water from broken pipes."

He gave a sharp laugh. "That was aviation fuel, my friend. Why do you think our eyes were watering so much?"

I was beginning to get the picture. I recalled my actions and got a bit light-headed. It was no damn wonder he thought I was a brave man, but it was bravery born of ignorance. If I had had the slightest inkling I was splashing around in gasoline, I would have left the house a hell of a lot faster than I entered it.

I remembered the doctor's warning to the firemen about one spark and the the whole place going up. I thought he was just exaggerating to scare them!

When the interview was concluded, the doctor looked much better, but I was a wreck. We shook hands at the door, and he said, "I'm going to write the sheriff a letter about your actions." He slapped me on the back. "That took a lot of guts."

I stared at him numbly, then turned and tottered to the elevator, accompanied by the imperturbable investigator.

Some days later, I did indeed receive a nice commendation from the sheriff, based on the doctor's letter. It described in explicit detail the risks I had taken while inside the gasoline-saturated house.

I didn't sleep well for weeks.

19

THE BARE FACTS

"Excuse me."

I looked up, slightly irritated at the interruption. I was right in the middle of one of my best war stories. Two teenage girls were standing beside our booth. Wearing bathing suits, their faces sun-reddened, sand still on their feet, they had obviously just come in from the beach.

"Yes, what can I do for you?" I asked.

Nervous and self-conscious, one stammered, "Well. . . uh, . . I mean, you see, . . . we want to report something." She glanced at her companion, who nodded.

"What do you want to report?"

The other girl stepped forward. "A violation of the law." Embarrassed by her outburst, she quickly stepped back.

I sighed, "Girls, you're going to have to be more specific. What kind of violation?"

They looked at each other, waiting for the other to speak. "You tell him," the bashful one said, "you saw her first."

"Yeah, but you wanted to stop here when you saw the police car."

I was getting impatient. Being accosted by citizens in coffee shops and restaurants is just part of the job when one is a uniformed law enforcement officer, but normally the complainants get to the point a lot quicker.

David Stanley, an auxiliary deputy, had joined me at Butler's Restaurant here on the beach. He had just spent the last 45 minutes directing traffic around a minor wreck. Hot and sweaty, he was happy to get something cool to drink.

He, too, was getting impatient with the girls. "Could one of you flip a coin or something and tell us what happened?"

They giggled, and finally, the braver of the two said, "Nudity."

David and I looked at each other. "Did you say, 'nudity'?" I asked.

She nodded. "Yes, and we don't think it's right."

"Who is nude?"

She gestured "Some woman down on the beach."

"How far?" David asked.

She thought about this for a moment. "It must be four or five miles, but it's hard to tell because of all the traffic."

"What was she doing?"

The girl flushed, "Nothing, really; she was just, just... NUDE. On the sand."

"I think she was sunbathing," her friend added.

Nude sunbathing. Not uncommon, but generally done in secluded locations. The girls indicated this woman was out in public, and public nudity could well constitute indecent exposure. If the exposure was occurring in front of minor children, it might even be a felony.

"We think it should be stopped," she said. "It's not right."

"We'll show you where she is," her friend offered. "You can just follow us."

I wasn't too eager to comply. For one thing, I figured at least a half-hour had elapsed since the two had first seen the nude sunbather. It would take another twenty minutes or so for us to pick our way through the heavy beach traffic. The odds of the woman still being on the beach, nude or clothed, were remote.

But we had no choice. These two guardians of the public

decency obviously did not intend to allow us to shirk our constituted responsibility. Besides, the conversation had been overheard by most of the patrons in the restaurant. We would have to go.

Muttering, David gulped down his Coke, and we followed the girls out of the restaurant.

On the way to the scene of the crime, we discussed the possibility of actually finding the woman. "I think she'll be long gone before we even get there," David said. "If she was even there in the first place."

I nodded. "I can't figure out why these two would go to all the trouble of reporting something like this. I mean, what's it to them? Even if the woman is still there, which I doubt, why do they care?"

David laughed, "Maybe their boyfriends are still back there admiring the view."

Fifteen minutes later the girls pulled into a parking area. "She's over there," one of them said, pointing toward the beach, "over that big sand dune."

"You're sure of that?" David asked.

She nodded. "We're going to leave now," her friend said. "We don't want to be here when you catch her." They scuttled back to their car and drove off.

"There's something fishy about all this," David said darkly. "Why wouldn't they stick around?"

"I don't know, but I think we've made a dry run."

We trudged up the dune, sand filling our shoes, sweat beginning to trickle down our faces. We reached the top and scanned the area. The beach was dotted with people frolicking in the water, lying on towels and blankets, and tossing frisbees. The sugar-white sand was dazzling in the bright sun and, in combination with the azure blue of the gulf and the creamy line of surf, presented a scene so achingly beautiful I had to stop to drink it all in.

"What's that over there?" David said, pointing.

I shaded my eyes. About a hundred yards to the right of us a knot of people were gathered. It seemed to be an all-male group, many of whom were taking pictures of something or someone on the sand. We were too far away to determine what it was.

David said, "You don't think. . . " He left the sentence unfinished.

We started toward the group, and several turned and strolled away as we approached. We walked up to them and, for the first time, got a clear view.

David sucked in his breath and said, "God almighty," in a reverent tone. I tried to talk, but the words caught in my throat. There on the sand, lying on a towel, was a beautiful dark-haired woman, her eyes closed. She had a tan that looked like a Coppertone ad. It was really an amazing tan, very even. All over. I could speak with some authority on this subject because, at the moment, she didn't have a stitch of clothing on.

In a semi-circle around her, the group of men talked quietly among themselves, snapped pictures, or just stared unabashedly. I didn't blame them. The woman had a body like a Playboy centerfold. We all stood there watching the regular rise and fall of her bountiful chest as she breathed. It was truly an amazing sight.

Then one of the men laughed, and I reluctantly came back to reality. The woman was breaking the law, and we were cops. We had to do something. I cleared my throat. "Uh, excuse me, ma'am."

The woman stirred and opened her eyes. She took in my uniform, and her eyes shifted as she noticed David standing, slack jawed and bug-eyed, beside me. I fully expected her to register some degree of shock or concern, but she simply said politely, "Yes, officer, what's the problem?"

I was more than a little nonplussed. "Ma'am, you can't sunbathe in the nude here."

"Where can I go?"

That threw me. "Ma'am, I don't know where you can go,

but you can't stay here on a public beach; it's against the law."
There were low boos and hisses from the crowd.

She sat up, and I felt faint. "Well, I tried to find a place where
I could be by myself, but people keep following me."

I tried to get my breathing under control. "I'm sorry, you'll
just have to find another place."

"All right, if I have to." She stood up and there was an
appreciative "oooooh" from the group, like the crowd noise
at a fireworks display. She slipped into as skimpy a pair of shorts
as I have ever seen and pulled a flimsy tank top over her head.

"I wasn't hurting anyone, was I?" she asked.

I turned toward her, then hurriedly looked away. The sight
of her barely clothed body was much more erotic than when she
was totally naked. "No, you weren't hurting anyone, but it is
against the law. What's your name?"

She gave me a dazzling smile, "It's Cynthia, what's yours?"

"Parker, Don Parker."

She extended her hand, and I shook it automatically. There
was a flurry of camera clicks, and I felt like an idiot. If one of
those pictures made it to the *News Journal*, I was a dead man.
I snatched my hand away.

"Thanks for being so nice about it, Don," she said, brushing
sand off her chest. I felt the sweat break out on my lip. I couldn't
take much more of this.

"Yes, well, you'll have to leave now." She picked up her
towel and strode off across the sand, long legs gleaming, jiggling
in all the appropriate places. At the top of the dune she turned
and waved to the crowd, who broke into applause. A second
later she disappeared from view.

Back in our car, we sat in stunned silence. Finally, David let
out a long breath. "We could have arrested her."

"Sure, but the paper would have had a field day." I laughed.
"Besides, how would we have searched her?"

He gazed dreamily into the distance, shaking his head slowly,
"Believe me, I'd have figured out a way."

20

DEATH OF A BEAGLE

Engine thundering, I sped along the twisting road. I was headed for a convenience store where the clerk was having trouble with a shoplifter. I was just the backup unit, but I didn't want to waste any time getting there. Since I was steaming along at about 80, so I had the blue lights on, but the roads were dry and traffic light, so I wasn't too concerned.

As I came out of a curve I saw two young boys on bikes on the other side of the road. I touched the siren once to make sure they saw me. At the wail, they slowed somewhat and watched me approach, fascinated by the sight of my speeding cruiser. As I got closer, I noticed a small beagle trotting along behind the bikes, nose to the ground, sniffing busily, oblivious to the commotion I was making.

The boys stopped as I drew abreast of them but their dog continued on. Suddenly, he made a sharp left turn, and crossed the road, directly in my path!

It was over in an instant. There was a sickening, thump-thump, as both front and rear wheels struck the dog. I was heartsick. I am fond of all animals, particularly dogs, and now, doubtless, I had killed one. I looked in the mirror. The still-twitching body of the poor beagle lay on the edge of the highway, the two boys standing over him.

I backed up to the gruesome scene. I could only imagine the traumatic effect on the two youngsters. For them to witness the brutal death of their beloved pet, crushed beneath the wheels of a hurtling cruiser car might well turn them into cop haters for life.

I felt sick. I knew in my heart there was nothing I could have done, but it didn't make me feel any better. Now I would have to provide some comfort for these two little boys. I, the one who had just killed their dog. The animal lay in the road, twitching now and then, a trickle of blood running from his mouth. It was a horrifying sight.

I turned to the boys. They were staring at the beagle and my heart went out to them. Two little tykes, possibly nine or ten years old, golden hair ruffled by the wind, two pairs of blue eyes riveted on their dying dog. As we watched in silence, the unfortunate animal shuddered, and a pool of urine began to puddle beneath him.

The taller of the two finally spoke, "Aw, neat! Did you see that Jimmie?"

"Yeah," Jimmie said enthusiastically, "He's peeing."

The dog jerked again, then lay still. "Boy, that was sharp." Jimmie said, "Did you see his leg, Josh?"

Josh held up his arm and gave a grotesque but accurate imitation of the dying dog's last movements. Both boys burst into laughter.

I began to feel that perhaps they would survive this tragedy without too much permanent damage.

"Who owns the dog?" I asked.

Both shrugged. "We just saw him up the road," Josh said. "We were trying to make him leave us alone."

"Yeah, but he wouldn't do it," Jimmie said, "until you came along." He started to giggle, and Josh punched him on the arm.

We looked at the dog. Several flies were greedily walking along its muzzle. "Oh, gross!" they cried in unison.

The dog had no collar, so I had the dispatcher notify the county animal shelter to pick up the body.

The boys helped me drag the late beagle off the road, and I headed back toward the convenience store. The last view I had of the scene was the sight of the two little boys, standing over the carcass of the dog, hoping it would twitch again.

21

HOW TO CREATE AN INTERNATIONAL INCIDENT

Siren wailing, I approached the intersection of Navy Boulevard and Old Corry Road, twisting my head like a fighter pilot, looking for oncoming traffic. It was clear, and I moved through cautiously, speeding up as I passed the traffic light. Cars ahead pulled to the side of the road, alerted by the flashing blue lights in the night sky and the scream of my siren.

I was one of several units enroute to a report of a silent alarm at a furniture store. We all loved silent alarms because we had a much better chance of actually catching a burglar inside a building, since he had not been frightened off by the sound of an audible alarm.

I was coming up on the Twinair Drive-in, and it looked as though a movie had just ended. Cars were coming out of the exits and turning onto Navy Boulevard. I was happy to see that most had halted at the sight of my cruiser.

Most, but not all. A large, four-door sedan was picking its way through the crowd of immobile automobiles, moving toward the highway. Surely he would stop when he saw me coming, but just to be on the safe side, I moved to the outside lane and slowed a little. The car crossed the two lanes of westbound traffic and moved into the median.

He was bound to see me now. The whole area was being

illuminated by the blinding blue flashes from my lights, and everyone within five miles must be wincing at the noise from my siren.

Majestically, the big car made a sweeping turn, crossing both lanes of traffic. I was horrified to see that at my present rate of travel the big car was going to squeeze me off the road. I had a choice: Either be sideswiped by the heavy sedan, or take to the shoulder of the road. I opted for the side of the road. The shoulder was gullied and washed out, and my sprinting cruiser was immediately turned into a bucking bronco as it hit the corrugated surface. Caroming around the front seat, I grimly held onto the wheel, tapping the brakes until I regained control. My heart began beating again.

My diminishing fear was replaced by rage at the stupidity of the driver, still proceeding serenely down Navy Boulevard, oblivious to my crash landing.

The silent alarm was forgotten as I went after the car. I quickly caught up with him and hung onto his bumper, rattling his back window with my siren until he finally pulled off the road. I stormed up to the driver's window, so angry my teeth were chattering.

A well dressed man in his 40's rolled the window down, the flashes from my blue lights reflecting off his tinted glasses. He was wearing an expensive suit, and his tie was secured with an old-fashioned diamond stick pin. He exuded a sense of money, from his carefully trimmed moustache to his manicured fingernails. A woman was on the passenger side, and another couple was in the back, but I only had eyes for the man who had run me off the road.

"May I be of asseeetance?" he asked, in heavily accented English.

"You sure as hell can." I said through clenched teeth, "Get out of the car."

He looked at me calmly, "I do not understand," he said, but I was already opening the door.

"I said," taking him firmly by the arm, "Get-Out-Of-The-Car!" I had his attention now. "Your driver's license, please."

He removed a large, rectangular wallet from his inside coat pocket and handed it to me. His photograph was on a fancy document decorated with a variety of stamps, seals, and ribbons.

"Very impressive, but I want your driver's license."

He pointed at the document, "Consular," he said, rolling the 'r', "diplomat."

I had no idea what he was talking about, but I did know he had run me off the road, and he hadn't produced a driver's license. That was enough for me. I grabbed his arm and started him toward my cruiser car, "You're under arrest."

"No arrest, no arrest," he said loudly. "Diplomat, immunity." There was a burst of Spanish from the occupants of the car, but no one got out. This was just as well. In my present state of mind, I would have happily loaded the whole bunch.

He was still protesting, "No arrest, no arrest," as I placed him in the back seat of my cruiser and closed the door. I felt much better. There's nothing like taking direct action against the object of your frustration to brighten your whole day.

I stood by my car studying the document he had given me. As far as I could tell, he was an employee of the Paraguayan Consulate. What he was doing in Pensacola attending a drive-in movie was a mystery. The more I thought about the situation, the more uncertain I became. Maybe I'd better check with the sergeant on this.

The silent alarm hadn't panned out, and he arrived in a few minutes.

Sergeant John Franklin Tyler was a 26 year veteran of the Escambia County Sheriff's Department and had managed to survive three different sheriffs. He was fast approaching retirement and was at the point in his career where he did not like to be unduly upset. The list of things that upset him was lengthy. It included the sheriff or chief deputy, complaining about the actions of one of the deputies on his shift; members of the news media wanting to quote him on something; deputies who damaged their cruiser cars by running them into hard objects; deputies who damaged soft objects, like people, by running into them with their cruiser cars; deputies who shot taxpayers without the most extreme provocation: in short, almost anything that would cause the slightest ripple on the calm, placid surface of his well-ordered existence.

There was one final thing which caused him to become particularly upset, and that was gung-ho young deputies who insisted on arresting what he regarded as "risky people." People like county commissioners, mayors, or, as I soon discovered, Paraguayan diplomats.

He pulled up behind my cruiser and got out of his car. "What's up?"

I pointed to my prisoner. "This clown ran me off the road right in front of the Twinair. I damn near broke an axle, and on top of that, he doesn't have a driver's license."

Sergeant Tyler was puzzled. This wasn't the kind of problem that required the personal attention of the shift commander. If I thought I had sufficient probable cause to make an arrest on what amounted to a rather simple traffic charge, he wasn't going to argue the point. There had to be more to this. He waited for the other shoe to drop.

I handed him the leather case. "He gave me this, but it doesn't look like a driver's license to me." Tyler opened the case and began to read. "He says he's a diplomat or something," I said. "He can hardly speak English."

A furrow of apprehension appeared on the sergeant's forehead. The more he read, the deeper the furrow became. He looked at me with a worried expression. "What, exactly, did he say?"

I waved my hand carelessly. "Oh, some nonsense about immunity or something. I didn't know what he was talking about."

He blinked in alarm and reread the document hastily. "Anyway," I continued, "he damn sure didn't produce a driver's, license so I. . ."

"Oh, my God," Tyler whispered, eyes wide with panic, "do you know who this guy is?"

I was feeling a little uneasy at his reaction. Sergeant Tyler was usually pretty steady. "Yeah, I know who he is. He's the guy who almost got me killed. He pulled out, right in. . ."

"He's a diplomat."

"So what?"

"So what?" he hissed, "Don't you know these guys have diplomatic immunity?"

"Yeah, he said that, but I. . . "

"And you arrested him?"

"I didn't know he. . . "

Beads of sweat glistened on his face. "Do you want to start an international incident?"

I gulped, "Of course not, Sarge. How was I to know he. . ."

But Tyler was no longer listening to me. Visions of his hard earned pension going up in smoke galvanized him into action. He opened the back door of my cruiser and helped the man out. With an ingratiating smile that didn't mask the terror in his eyes, Tyler handed him the wallet. "There's been a mistake, sir. You're free to go."

"No arrest, no arrest," the man said. "Diplomat. Immunity."

The sergeant bobbed his head up and down in enthusiastic agreement. "Oh, no, sir, no arrest." He fluttered around him, doing everything but dusting him off. He gestured toward the man's car. "You're free to go, we're sorry about the mistake."

The man edged away from my cruiser, watching me apprehensively. "Diplomat," he said.

"Right, diplomat, no arrest," the Sergeant said, guiding him toward the big sedan. Tyler quickly opened the door like a chauffeur. I thought for a moment he was going to curtsy. The man got in.

There was a lengthy conversation between him and his companions while Tyler stood by, grinning and sweating. Finally, one of them handed something to the diplomat, who held it out to Tyler. He took it, nodding agreeably.

It was a twenty dollar bill.

Sergeant Tyler let out a strangled yelp, tossed the money into the car, and jumped back about six feet. The driver caught the bill as it fluttered to the seat and extended it again.

"No, no, no," Tyler said, holding his hands in front of him and backing away, like Dracula shielding himself from a crucifix. Thoroughly spooked now, he scuttled back to his own car. The diplomat shrugged, closed the door, and drove away.

Tyler drew a shuddering breath. "My God," he said shakily, "did you see that?"

I laughed, "Aw, he wasn't trying to bribe you, sarge. I think he just wanted to give you a present."

Tyler whirled on me angrily, and my laughter died. "It's not funny, Parker. You could have caused the department serious embarrassment." (Translation: You could have caused ME serious embarrassment.)

Actually, I had been a little nervous myself, but I felt much better now that the guy was gone. Besides, I reflected as I got back in my car, how many deputies ever have the opportunity to cause an international incident all by themselves?

22

TRAFFIC STOP #2

I had been following the car for at least a half a mile trying to get it stopped, my blue lights flashing, the siren yelping and howling; but there had been no response from the driver. We continued to move down the road at a sedate 27 miles per hour, well below the posted limit of 45.

I could see the driver clearly, peeping over the steering wheel, thin, snow-white hair framing his wrinkled face. He was concentrating ferociously on the job of piloting his battered old station wagon. With both hands clamped tightly on the wheel, he stared straight ahead, watching the road intently. The station wagon drifted across the center line, then back the other way.

It was this erratic driving plus his slow speed which first attracted my attention. The old gentleman passed in front of me while I waited at a stop sign. A procession of cars trailed behind him, and from the amount of horn blowing and fist shaking, I could tell the drivers were not pleased. Some of the more impatient ones swung out to pass, but quickly lost their enthusiasm for this idea when the big car moved slowly into their lane.

I pulled into the procession and leapfrogged to the front using my siren and blue lights. I was soon behind the station wagon, but there I stayed. The car's excursions across the center line at frequent but unpredictable moments kept me from pulling up beside him.

He was driving reasonably well, negotiating turns with no major problems, other than scaring the hell out of several oncoming drivers who were forced to dive for the side of the road when the station wagon swayed into their lane.

I waited until the car started sashaying to the right, then shot around it, pulling in front of him to let him get a good look at all the blue lights. I swung back into the oncoming lane and let him catch up. When he looked over at me, I started vigorously waving him to the side of the road. After a long interval, the station wagon began to slow. The car eased off the pavement and came to a stop. I pulled in behind him.

The old man watched me approach without the slightest sign of nervousness. Rolling the window down, he peered up at me, smiling benignly. My suspicions were that he was drunk, but there was no indication of it. No smell of beer or whiskey, no bottles or cans visible, and his eyes seemed bright and alert.

"May I see your driver's license, please?" I said.

He did not react but continued to look at me with pleasant interest.

"May I see your driver's license, please?" I repeated, louder this time.

He put one hand behind his ear, "Eh?"

"MAY I SEE YOUR DRIVER'S LICENSE, PLEASE?"

A smile of understanding illuminated his face, and he nodded happily. "Ain't got one," he said cheerfully.

Great. "Where is it?" I shouted.

"Eh?"

"WHERE IS YOUR LICENSE?" I roared.

"They took it away."

"Who did?" He cupped his ear again. "WHO TOOK YOUR LICENSE?"

He pondered this a moment. "I reckon it was them boys from the state."

This could only mean his license had been suspended or revoked, and someone from the State Department of Motor Vehicles had picked it up.

I took a deep breath. "HOW LONG AGO?" I shouted, a little hoarsely now.

"I reckon it was about ten years ago."

"Ten years?" I said incredulously.

"Eh?"

"Ten...Oh, never mind."

"Eh?"

"I SAID, 'NEVER MIND'!" My throat was beginning to hurt.

Luckily, he did have some identification. His name was Franklin Archer, and he was 79. I had the radio room call his home, and a very worried daughter said she would be right there.

She arrived in a short time, driven by a neighbor. An anxious-looking plump woman, gray hair straggling from a hastily constructed bun, she must have been close to 60 herself. She approached me hurriedly. "Is he all right?"

"I'm sure he's fine."

She wrung her hands. "I was taking a nap, and when I got up, he was gone. He hasn't had a driver's license in years, but he still thinks he can drive. I'm scared to death he's going to get himself killed or hurt someone else." She shook her head. "He takes my car keys if I leave them lying around."

We walked toward the station wagon. "You know he's deaf as a post," she said.

"So I found out."

She cupped her ear, "Pardon me?"

"SO I FOUND OUT," I screamed. She flinched and covered her ear.

I was mortified. "I'm so sorry, ma'am; it's just that I've been talking to your father for the past 20 minutes."

"That's quite all right," she said, but I noticed she moved away from me.

I helped Mr. Archer out of the car and walked him around to the passenger side. His daughter followed. "Daddy, why do you do this?" she wailed. "I get so frightened."

He stood there placidly, smiling uncomprehendingly as the unheard words swirled around him.

She turned to me. "Are you going to put him in jail?" she asked fearfully.

I had to smile. "I don't think that will be necessary. He didn't cause an accident, and he certainly doesn't belong in jail."

"Oh, thank you, thank you!" she was almost in tears.

I helped her father into the car. He stuck out his hand, and I shook it. "Good luck, Mr. Archer."

"Eh?"

"GOOD LUCK!" I bellowed.

He frowned, "You don't have to shout, young fella."

23

HOW TO TESTIFY
IN COURT

"State your name, please."

"Don Parker."

"Where are you employed, Mr. Parker?"

"The Escambia County Sheriff's Department."

"How long have you been so employed?"

"Four years, four months."

"Where are you currently assigned?"

"I'm assigned to the uniformed patrol division."

"And what is the nature of your duties?"

"I'm a uniformed deputy sheriff: I drive a marked cruiser car, answer calls for assistance, make arrests, write traffic citations and investigate crimes."

"And were you so engaged on the night of February 24th?"

"I was."

"And did you have occasion to come into contact with the defendant, James Allen Simpson?"

"I did."

"And what was the nature of that contact?"

"I saw him being booked at the county jail on a charge of armed robbery." The prosecutor looked confused. But he wasn't alone. I was a little confused myself, wondering why I had been subpoenaed to testify in a case about which I knew so little. I had seen the defendant for perhaps 15 minutes when he was brought into the jail while I was finishing up the paperwork on a drunk driver.

The prosecutor extracted the arrest report from the file and scanned it a moment. "Deputy Parker, did you not first see the defendant, James Allen Simpson, when you stopped the vehicle he was driving at approximately 7:58 P.M.?"

"No, sir."

His eyes widened. He stepped to the witness box and extended the arrest report. "Deputy Parker, do you recognize this report?"

It was totally unfamiliar. "No, sir, I do not."

"Deputy Parker," he said in an exasperated tone, "is this not your signature on the arrest report of the defendant, James Allen Simpson?"

I studied the name for a moment and then realized what had happened. However, there was nothing I could do to prevent the irritated prosecutor from suffering major embarrassment. "No, sir," I said, "it's Don Powell's signature."

He stared at me uncomprehendingly. "Don Powell?" he repeated.

"Yes, sir. I'm Don Parker. Don Powell was the arresting officer on that case; I saw him booking the defendant that night." There were titters from the spectators as the color drained from the prosecutor's face. "I think there's been a mistake," I said gently.

He looked at the name on the report and realized the error. Some poor secretary was probably going to catch hell for this one. He turned to the judge. "Your honor, there's obviously been some mis-communication here; the witness is excused."

Laughter followed me from the room.

24

COPS ARE HELPFUL PEOPLE
PART 1

Rain. Slanting down from the cold November sky. Rattling like buckshot against the side of my car, drumming insistently on the roof, trying to get at me. It was close to two in the morning, and I was on patrol, driving cautiously along a partially submerged highway. With such terrible weather, there was little traffic and few calls, for which I had been profoundly grateful.

It was warm and dry inside my cruiser. The heater bathed my feet and legs in warmth and the steady thump-thump-thump of the windshield wipers provided a comforting rhythm as I guided the car around the deep puddles. The radio had been silent for at least a half-hour, except when it sizzled with static as a streak of lightning tore across the sky. It was in the forties outside, and the strong wind rocked the car. I snuggled into my heavy coat, glad to be inside. Now, if it would just stay quiet.

As I approached an overpass, I saw the glow of tail lights ahead. I drew closer and saw a man wrapped in a flimsy jacket trying to change a tire on a shiny blue Cadillac. He had the big car up on the jack, and the spare tire rested against the rear bumper, waiting to replace the flat. A particularly strong gust of wind drenched him with rain, and he paused to wipe the water from his face. The narrow overpass was a poor shelter from a storm like this. He didn't even look up as I approached, but took advantage of the watery glare of my headlights to loosen another lug nut.

I found myself on the horns of a painful dilemma. If I stopped to help, I, too, would be rapidly soaked and frozen by the rainstorm. No raincoat made was going to keep out the water on a night like this.

On the other hand, if I drove by without stopping, it was likely he would never be the wiser. His back was to the road, and he was probably so miserable by now he wouldn't have noticed the *U.S.S. New Jersey* go by. If I didn't stop, no one would ever know.

Except me.

Of course, I already knew I was going to stop. I groaned, cursing my soft streak, but there was nothing else to do. I didn't become a cop so I could ignore people in distress.

I pulled in behind the Cadillac, lighting up the area with my spotlight. I also switched on the blue lights. I didn't want some drunk running over me in the blowing darkness. I did what I could to prepare for the coming onslaught by buttoning my coat all the way up, turning my collar up to my ears, and snugging my hat tightly to my head. I took a deep breath and stepped into the maelstrom.

After three steps, I realized how pitifully inadequate my feeble attempts had been to stay dry. I was sloshing through ankle-deep water which filled my shoes and soaked me to the knees. The wind was behind me, but the effect was the same as someone turning a hose on the back of my neck. Freezing water cascaded merrily down my back, racing for my knees. It was just as bad as I had feared.

The tire changer seemed frozen in place as he squinted into the lights of my cruiser. He was younger than I realized, with a mass of sodden dark brown hair. Water dripped steadily from a matching mustache. He stared at me, the tire tool held motionless in front of him. Cops have this effect on some people, so I gave him a big smile and said with as much heartiness as

I could muster, "Having some tire trouble?"

"Flat tire," he croaked.

I crouched beside him, and my coat parted, allowing the slashing rain to attack my exposed pants. They were soaked through in an instant. "Maybe I can help," I said.

"Help?" he asked tonelessly. He made no move to resume his labors.

There was something distinctly odd about his behavior. I expect to startle people occasionally, perhaps even make them uneasy, but this guy was really spooked. My built-in law enforcement radar sounded an alarm. "I thought you could use the light from my car to get that tire changed," I said, pointing to the still-attached flat.

This seemed to galvanize him into action and he became a blur of activity as he began removing the lug nuts again. I stood up, hoping to make the rain work a little harder at getting me wet. As far as I could tell, there was a small portion on the front of my shirt that was not soaked yet. I leaned forward, trying to protect it.

The flat was soon off, and the young man almost ran the spare tire into place. I didn't blame him. Even with all my protective gear, I was stiff with cold. I was surprised he could even move. We threw the flat into the trunk, and he turned to me. "How much do I owe you?" he asked, pulling out his dripping wallet.

I recoiled, "We don't accept money for doing our job."

"Well, at least let me write the sheriff a letter and tell him how nice you were."

Nothing wrong with that idea. "I guess that would be all right."

He fished around in the pocket of his jacket and extracted a ballpoint and a damp pack of cigarettes. After several attempts, he finally got the pen to write and carefully copied my name on the back of the package.

He was still acting very nervous. Damn it, there was something wrong here, but what? I had already looked inside the car while he was working on the tire but had not seen anything suspicious. It was always possible he was wanted for a crime, but that wasn't the feeling I was getting. My cop hunch said it was something else.

As we stood there in the downpour I happened to glance at the license plate, and suddenly, I knew! The tag had expired. The validation sticker said October, and this was already November the seventh. No wonder he was acting so nervous.

I felt so good at solving the mystery I almost smiled, but I decided to string the guy along a bit more. "Well, have a safe trip home," I said casually.

He gave me a wan smile, "I will, and thanks for all your help." He opened the door of the Cadillac.

"Wait a minute," I said sharply, "there's one more thing." He turned toward me, eyes wide with apprehension. "Step back here a minute, please." I was really playing the role now, snapping out my commands tautly. Woodenly, he obeyed and stood beside me quivering. "How do you explain that?" I asked, pointing at the expired tag.

His face collapsed, and I thought he was going to cry. I had gone too far. "Hey, look," I said hastily, "it's just an expired tag. I'm not going to give you a ticket, but you better take care of it before some state trooper gets you."

"Expired tag?" he whispered.

"Yes, expired tag. I know you were hoping I wouldn't notice, but I've been in this game a long time, and I could tell you were a little nervous." I slapped him on the back. "Now get on out of here before we both freeze to death."

He leaped for the car. "Oh, I will, sir, I will, and thank you again." The expensive engine rumbled to life, and the Cadillac disappeared into the rainy darkness.

I squished back to my cruiser, straining to see through my rain-speckled glasses. Back in the blessed warmth of my car, I removed my wide brimmed hat and dumped about a pint of icy water into my lap. I was soaked and freezing, but I had to chuckle. It was almost worth it to see the expression on that poor guy's face when I pointed out the expired tag. He thought he was caught for sure.

Thirty minutes later the radio crackled. "Headquarters to all units, standby for a stolen vehicle broadcast."

I pulled to the side of the road to better copy the description of the car.

"Back to all units, be on the lookout for a late model Cadillac Fleetwood, dark blue in color, stolen within the hour, direction of travel unknown. Tag and VIN (Vehicle Identification Number) to follow."

Suddenly, my mouth was very dry, and a strange hollow sensation filled my stomach.

In a moment, the precise, measured tones of the dispatcher gave us the license plate number and the VIN. I copied the two numbers hopelessly as an overwhelming dread washed over me. It was the same car.

He had a big enough head start to be out of the state by now. I pounded the steering wheel in fury. Why hadn't I run a registration check on the tag or at least asked for some identification? He was probably still laughing at me, the friendly cop who helps car thieves change flat tires in the rain.

I debated my next move. If I admitted I had actually helped the thief make his getaway, my gleeful co-workers would make me suffer for the rest of my life.

On the other hand, my description of the driver and the direction of travel of the Cadillac was valuable information that needed to be passed on.

After several minutes of agonizing, I finally decided on a course of action. I would admit only that I had seen a car fitting the description of the one stolen, while it was stopped at a red light. Naturally, I would have been able to see enough of the driver to give a brief description, and naturally, I would have remembered which way the car headed.

I proceeded with my plan, but when I finished, a chilling

thought clutched at me: What would happen if one of our guys located the car and arrested the thief? No doubt, he would brag long and loud about the deputy who helped him change the tire. If that happened my life would be over.

The remaining three hours of the shift dragged by with glacial slowness. Every time one of my buddies made a traffic stop, my heart quit beating until I was sure it wasn't the Cadillac. Fortunately, for me, anyway, no one apprehended the guy.

I suppose that some good did come out of this incident. For the rest of my career, whenever I stopped to assist a stranded motorist, I did everything but give them a lie detector test.

25
COPS ARE HELPFUL PEOPLE PART 2

Wintertime in Florida, particularly south Florida, is very pleasant. The balmy winds, the bright sun, and the toasty warm temperatures combine to make it the nicest time of the year. It's the very image of Florida, the one that sends tourism officials into transports of joy as they sing the lyrical praises of our fair state.

Yes, the weather in Florida is very pleasant. In the winter.

In the summer, however, it is a different story, because summers in Florida are not pleasant. It is said that some people consider a summer in Florida punishment for the sins they committed during the winter. In the summer, that soft sun of winter now beats down with unremitting fury, turning asphalt streets into sticky traps for the unwary and browning any verdant lawns not served by a sprinkler system. Temperatures stay in the high 90's during most of June, July, August, and September. But it is not the temperature which causes undue comment. It's the humidity.

Now the word "humidity" is an innocuous one denoting the amount of moisture in the air. There are all sorts of scientific explanations for how this occurs, but any lengthy discussion of the subject puts all but meteorologists into deep comas. To the rest of the world, humidity is just something the weather man

118

talks about on the evening news.

Not in Florida.

In Florida, in the summer, you can actually see humidity. It is a shimmering, gauze-like haze that hangs in the air. Do not mistake it for atmospheric pollution. This is not the noxious, yellowish smog of big cities; it is simply the air itself, bulging with water vapor.

Not only can you see humidity in the summer, you can feel it. Walking outside at noon in August is akin to taking a stroll through a sauna. Of course, in a sauna you are likely to be wearing only a towel. On the streets of a Florida city, you will probably have on a lot more clothing. Therefore, you will sweat just like in a sauna, but you won't be dressed for it.

First-time visitors to the Sunshine State step from the crisp coolness of their air-conditioned 727's and DC-10's into the steamy inferno of a Florida summer and think someone is playing a cruel trick on them. The hot, still air, so oppressively heavy, is like trying to breathe Jello. They can be forgiven if they stumble down the steps, shielding their eyes from the blazing sun, gasping that they can't breathe.

There is only one occasion when conditions exceed even the horror of having both the temperature and the humidity in the 90's. That is the short interval following a midday rain shower.

A brief rain does nothing except add even more moisture to the already saturated air. When the storm passes, whatever cooling has taken place is obliterated the instant the sun comes out again. Steam rises in clouds from the hot pavement, creating a knee-high fog bank which lasts until all the puddles evaporate. Conditions like this can make even a native cringe. Visitors are appalled when they discover there are thunderstorms every afternoon during the summer.

It was on just such a day, a blazing August afternoon, that I had yet another opportunity to exercise my law enforcement intuition.

A thunderstorm had passed, and the air was steamy. After

booking a prisoner at the jail, I returned to my car, drenched with sweat from just the short walk across the parking lot. I pulled out of the driveway with all the air conditioning vents aimed at my face, greedily drinking in the blasts of cool air.

I had only gone a block or so when I saw her. A tall girl, about 16 or 17, wearing a red and white blouse and faded jeans. She was barefoot, but that was not what attracted my attention. What caused me to snap my head around in amazement was the fact she was running down the sidewalk by the juvenile detention center. Running. In that blast-furnace heat.

Now I figured there would only be two reasons why a girl would exert herself to that extent: (1) she was insane, or (2) she had a problem.

As I drew alongside her, I had the chance to look her over. She didn't appear insane. My law enforcement alarm system started clanging in my head, and little red warning flags began going up. There was something wrong here.

I steered for the curb and rolled down the passenger side window. The sound of my approach was covered by the rumble of a passing truck, so I was beside her before she was aware of me. "Anything wrong, Miss?" I shouted.

She swerved off the sidewalk, eyes wide with panic.

"Hey, take it easy," I yelled. "I'm not going to hurt you, I just want to know if anything is wrong."

She slowed a little, but she was still making pretty good time. She watched me warily as I kept pace with her, and after a moment she puffed, "Yeah, there's something . . wrong . . . I'm late . . . for the . . . bus."

Always the helpful cop, I asked solicitously, "Can I give you a lift?"

She shook her head and drops of perspiration flew. "No thanks, . . just . . . up to the . . . corner."

She had only a half a block to go. I waved farewell and speeded up, glad to be able to close the window and save my air-conditioning. I came to the intersection and turned right.

I was satisfied. Although essentially a false alarm, I felt I had read the situation correctly. That old cop hunch was right on the money. No normal person would be running on a day like this without a good reason. Late for the bus. Well, I knew it had to be something. I glanced in the mirror, expecting to see the girl standing on the corner. I looked again. Odd, I didn't see her, but traffic was heavy, and I quickly forgot about the barefoot runner as I maneuvered in the stream of rushing cars.

Two traffic lights later, I got a call.

"Headquarters to 109."

I keyed the microphone. "Go ahead, I'm on Pace Boulevard."

"10-4, 109, contact the intake counselor at the juvenile detention center. They had a white female juvenile go out the window on them."

A cold wind passed through me. It couldn't be. Uh...did they give a description, headquarters?"

"10-4," she replied promptly, "White female, 16 years old, shoulder-length brown hair, red-and-white shirt, blue jeans, barefooted. Last seen headed toward Leonard Street."

God, no! I had been close enough to touch her.

"109, did you copy?"

I writhed in embarrassment. I had made a complete fool of myself. Again.

"109, did you copy?" she said insistently.

"10-4," I said weakly, "I'll be enroute."

The intake counselor, a heavyset black woman with thick glasses, was hopping mad. "I chased that girl all the way to Leonard Street, but I'm no kid." This was easy to see. "I turned my back for a minute, and she was gone." She glared at me, "But you know what makes me furious?"

"What's that, ma'am?"

She pointed at my cruiser. "I saw one of your deputy cars driving along beside her, and the stupid cop didn't do a thing."

I could feel the color rising in my cheeks, and I ducked my head, writing busily.

"I was yelling and screaming, and he didn't even slow down."
I cleared my throat. "Well, maybe he didn't see her."

"Oh, he saw her all right," she said emphatically. He was right there beside her for about a block. I couldn't believe it!"

"Yes . . . well, I better get out and start looking for her." I was backing toward my car.

"I just wish I knew who that cop was, because I'd sure give him a piece of my mind." She was breathing hard. "Why in the hell did he think she was running, anyway?"

"Well, I expect he..."

"Maybe he thought she was jogging," she said mockingly.

"Did you get the number of the cruiser car?" I was taking a chance, but I had to know.

She pondered this for a while, as cold sweat prickled my forehead. Finally she shook her head. "No, I didn't think to look."

I started breathing once more. "I've got to go, so if..."

"But I'm sure I'd recognize him," she interjected. I ducked my head again.

I promised I would do what I could to find the girl.

"You ain't gonna catch that one," she hollered as I drove off. "She can run like a deer."

26

HOW TO ARREST A MURDER SUSPECT

It started, as many bar fights start, over a woman. She had been living with a man for some time, but they had an argument, and she left in a huff. She went to the local bar to seek comfort and sympathy which she soon found in abundance.

Accepting a beer from a man who recognized her unhappiness, she told him of her troubles. She accepted several more beers and before long was assuring her friend that she found him most attractive and could not for the life of her imagine why she had taken up with her now ex-boyfriend in the first place.

This was music to the ears of her benefactor. He was 32 years older than she, a thin, stooped man with a bad back that had forced him into a disability retirement. Not exactly a whiz with the ladies, his head was swimming at the thought of getting something going with this sweet, misunderstood young thing.

Just as he was about to suggest they sample the beer at his place, in walked the ex-boyfriend. As might be expected, he was less than thrilled to find her making goo-goo eyes at someone old enough to be her grandfather.

He jerked her to her feet and proceeded to give her a piece of his mind, ignoring his competition. Naturally, this was an insult the older man could not ignore. Fired by the alcohol coursing through his veins and filled with righteous indignation, he ordered the oaf to unhand his new love.

Unfortunately, righteous indignation was not much protection against someone 30 years younger and 60 pounds heavier. The boyfriend casually backhanded the man, sending him sprawling.

Reminded of his tendency to get physical when angry, the girl promptly fell back in love, and the two of them strolled to the bar to drink to their newfound happiness. Bruised and humiliated, the older man limped from the beer joint and went home, nursing his battered ego.

That should have been the end of it, but it wasn't. A half-hour later he returned to the bar and stood outside, yelling at his opponent to come outside and fight like a man. The boyfriend ignored the taunts for a while, but when some of the patrons started to laugh, he got mad and charged out the door to teach the old man a lesson.

It was a mistake.

As his foot hit the ground, there was an explosion, and he was driven backwards by a charge of buckshot which caught him square in the chest. Although mortally wounded, he tried to rise and was knocked down again by another blast, which killed him. Honor satisfied, the old man shouldered his shotgun and walked home.

I was one of several deputies dispatched to the shooting. Information was sketchy, but the terrified bartender made it clear the victim was in bad shape. The dispatcher said an ambulance was on the way, but there was no information as to the identity of the assailant.

I had been to the bar many times over the past few years, investigating everything from dice games to murders. I took a shortcut through a residential area and was steaming down the street when I saw something strange. A block or so ahead, a man was standing by the side of the road waving to me, and he was holding a shotgun. The butt was on the ground, and he had a grip on the end of the barrel. Although he made no hostile moves, I was understandably nervous as I pulled up beside him.

"I'm the one you're looking for," he said as I stepped from my car. At that point, I only knew there had been a shooting at the bar.

"Were you the one who did the shooting?" I asked. He nodded and handed me the shotgun, which I gingerly placed on the front seat. I read him his rights while he stood quietly, arms extended, waiting for me to handcuff him.

This whole time the dispatchers were jabbering away, giving a description of the suspect and a direction of travel. There was so much talking going on I couldn't tell them I already had the man in custody.

I put him in the back, and we headed toward the scene of the murder. I asked him why he shot the man. His eyes met mine in the rear-view mirror, and he said simply, "I had to. He knocked me down in front of my woman."

27

THE SAGA OF WINSTON
THE BULLDOG

I was sure I must have misunderstood the dispatcher. "You want me to do what?"

"Contact a lady in the south parking lot of the Holiday Inn," she said again, "and assist her in getting a bulldog out of her car."

"A bulldog?"

"10-4."

I have been dispatched to a lot of strange calls in my time, but this sounded as though it might set a record. I wondered how a bulldog got in her car in the first place. I also wondered what I was going to do with the bulldog when I got him (or her) out of the car.

Oh, well. It had been a slow night. I needed some excitement.

I pulled into the parking lot of the Holiday Inn and saw a well-dressed, matronly woman about 50 standing beside a Lincoln Town Car. The passenger door was open, and a dim shape moved around the front seat. The bulldog, no doubt.

"Thank you for responding to my call so promptly," she said as I stepped from my car. She had a pronounced British accent.

"What seems to be the problem, ma'am?"

She sighed, "It's my dog, Winston. I can't seem to get him out of my auto. I was hoping you could assist me."

"Why won't he get out of the car?"

"It's because of the veterinarian."

I looked around. We seemed to be the only ones in the parking lot. "I beg your pardon?"

She went on to explain that, when the dog was a puppy, the only time she put him in the car was when he had to go to the vet's, where he invariably got a shot. It didn't take long for him to associate getting out of the car at strange places with someone sticking a needle in him. "Since we've been on this trip, I've had nothing but trouble trying to get him out of the car," she concluded.

"How have you gotten him out before?"

"Oh, I usually get a few stout lads like yourself, and they eventually manage to pull him out. Once his feet hit the ground, he's gentle as a lamb."

I stared at her. "Does he ever bite?"

"Oh, he's nipped a few of them." My eyes widened, and she continued hastily, "But no one's ever really been hurt."

I had a difficult time imagining how a full-grown bulldog would "nip" someone. Most of the bulldogs I had seen were capable of removing an entire leg with one bite.

I studied the massive animal through the window. He seemed peaceful enough. I stepped to the door and bent down to get a closer look. Winston let out a snarl of rage and charged across the seat, barking thunderously, and suddenly, I was face to face with about 200 teeth. I yelped and made a graceful leap backwards, ending up on the hood of my cruiser. I was almost to the roof before I realized the dog was not pursuing me.

"Oh, dear," the lady said, twisting her hands, "I hope he didn't frighten you."

I clung to the siren. "Oh, no, ma'am. I just remembered I needed to check the bulbs in my blue lights." I climbed down from my perch slowly, watching the open door, but the dog made no attempt to leave the car. I edged toward the vehicle, prepared to beat a hasty retreat. Winston watched me suspiciously; a low rumble deep in his throat gradually increased in volume the closer I got. I stopped, and the noise abated. For the first time, I noticed the leash attached to his collar. "Ma'am, couldn't you just pull him out of the car by the leash?"

"Goodness knows I've tried, but he's just too strong for me." She slid into the front seat, and Winston rubbed his huge head against her arm, snuffling happily as she scratched his ears. She untangled the leash and stepped out, tugging. Instantly, Winston dug his feet into the upholstery, leaning back. The collar tightened, and his eyes bugged out slightly, but he didn't move an inch, even though she was pulling hard.

"Could I try?"

"Certainly," she puffed, slightly out of breath. I took the leash gingerly, ready to jump for the roof if Winston came after me, but he didn't move. I pulled, gently at first, then harder. It was like pulling on a tree. Winston's eyes protruded, his breath came in rasping gurgles, but he hardly moved. The animal was incredibly strong. But I was stronger. In spite of his reluctance, I was slowly dragging him across the seat, an inch at a time. A few more feet and I was going to have him out of the car, which was what I wanted. I thought. There was a loud pop, and I crashed backward into my car. The leash had broken.

Winston returned to his spot on the seat, snorting a little but unharmed.

Now what was I going to do? I sure as hell wasn't going to try and grab that walking bear trap with my hands. I opened the trunk of my car, hoping I had some rope. I didn't find any rope, but I did find my umbrella, which had a curved handle.

I held it up. "Ma'am, if you'll hook the handle under his collar, I'll try to pull him out."

"Do you think you can?"

I sighed, "Well, if this doesn't work, the only thing left for me to do is shoot him."

An expression of such horror crossed her face that I quickly added, "I'm just kidding."

She took the umbrella and sat down in the front seat again. Winston allowed himself to be petted and stroked and never felt the umbrella being hooked under his collar. As soon as it was secure, I edged up to the car. Winston was immediately alert, a low growl indicating he knew I was out there. "It's all right, Winnie," the woman cooed. "He won't hurt you. Mummy wants you to get out of the car like a good boy." Winnie was having none of it. His tiny eyes followed my every move.

"You can get out now, ma'am, just hold onto the end of the umbrella for me."

She did as I instructed, but the instant he felt the tug at his collar, Winston braced his legs against the seat and leaned back. The woman stepped aside, and I darted in behind her, grabbing the umbrella. Winston let out a roar and started across the seat. I yanked on the end, hoping I could use his momentum to help get him out of the car. It didn't work.

Winston put on the brakes and backed up so fast he pulled me halfway into the car. I hauled on the umbrella, and Winston began to move slowly across the seat, toenails digging furrows in the fabric. Snorting, gasping, and growling, Winston fought every inch of the way, but he was losing. Realizing the battle was going against him, he twisted in his collar and attacked the umbrella, biting savagely at the thing which had a hold of him. Spittle flew as he worked it over, but I hung on grimly, glad it wasn't my arm he was venting his wrath on.

With only a foot or so left, Winston gave the umbrella a particularly hard bite. There was a "Fwoomp," and it popped open. It startled both of us, but my surprise changed to rage when I saw my umbrella was now a ragged, tattered ruin. Two ribs were broken, the handle was splintered and scored, and the fabric looked as though it had been shredded by buckshot. "Damn you, Winston!" I yelled. I gave a tremendous jerk, and the still-snarling bulldog sailed out of the car and landed on the pavement.

The woman was all over him immediately. "Oh, Winnie, there's a good boy. Now that wasn't so bad, was it? Mummy's so glad to have you out of that nasty old car.'' She unhooked the mangled umbrella and cast it aside. Winston waddled over to the grass, lifted his leg, and held that position for what seemed like five minutes as he proceeded to irrigate most of the lawn. The woman colored slightly. "He always does that when we first get him out," she said apologetically.

I was still watching Winston pump ship, wondering if his leg were going to cramp.

"I can't thank you enough for all your help," she said, "I could never have gotten him out by myself." She rummaged around in her handbag and extracted a pen and a small notebook. "You must give me your mailing address. I intend to see you are commended for your performance."

"That's not necessary, ma'am. I was glad to do it."

"Oh, no, I insist." I gave her the information, and after thanking me profusely again, she and Winston left to take a walk around the parking lot.

Sorrowfully, I disposed of the heroic remains of my poor umbrella, killed in the line of duty. I wrote a short report and went back to work.

She did, indeed, write me a very nice letter, on lilac-scented stationary, her flowing, ornate handwriting beautiful to behold. I never had the guts to turn it in. I could just imagine how my co-workers would react if I got a letter from the sheriff commending me for pulling a bulldog out of a car.

28

ATTACK OF THE LAWN CHAIR

It's a fact that men and women busily engaged in being unpleasant with each other sometimes turn on the cops sent to break up their fun, but this is the exception rather than the rule. It has happened to me a few times, and the incident I remember best occurred on one of the coldest nights of the year.

A deputy named Richard Lowery and I were sent to investigate a report of a woman screaming. The house was located in a seedy section of town where the yards were full of rusting cars on concrete blocks. This particular neighborhood was not exactly supportive of law enforcement, and the residents had been known to gather in large groups when we were in the area. If these folks disagreed with our methods, they were not shy about expressing their unhappiness. On more than one occasion, I had fought pitched battles in that very area.

But tonight I didn't think we would have much of an audience. The temperature was in the low twenties, and the wind was blowing hard. Not exactly the kind of weather to draw a crowd. I had to remind myself we were actually in Florida.

Although Lowery was considerably senior to me, I had been assigned the call, so I was theoretically in charge. Barring some major problem, I would make the decision how the call was to be handled, and I would do the paperwork.

YOU'RE UNDER ARREST

We found the house quickly, since it was one of the few that had a visible street number. It was a single-story clapboard structure, once white but now faded to a mottled grey. The yard was relatively neat, and there were no bursting garbage bags as in most of the others.

The two of us stood for a moment in the biting wind, looking and listening for signs of trouble, but all was quiet. Hunched against the cold in our heavy coats, we approached the door cautiously, hands resting on the butts of our service revolvers. Vague calls like "woman screaming" tend to make us nervous.

I knocked, and a soft voice called, "Who's there?"

"Sheriff's department," I said. There was a metallic rattle as the chain was removed, and the door opened. We faced an attractive brunette, wearing a pink housecoat belted at the waist. Her tear-stained face told me we had the right house. "Someone reported a woman screaming," I said. "Was that you?"

Tears welled up in her eyes and spilled down her cheeks. "Yes, it was me," she sobbed. "Come in."

We stepped into the low-ceilinged living room of a sparsely-furnished home. The windows were covered with sheets of plastic which crinkled and billowed as the wind gusted. A small gas heater hissed in one corner. It made the room oppressively warm to me, after the frigid air outside.

A stocky man wearing an embroidered cowboy shirt, jeans, and boots with pointed toes, sat on the couch. Lowery shifted his position slightly, to give himself some room so he could move in either direction if he had to. The guy looked unhappy but was peaceful, at least so far. I hoped he'd stay that way. He was a big man, and I didn't relish the idea of having to fight him in such a confined space.

The woman was still crying quietly. "What's the trouble, ma'am?" I said, opening my notebook.

She gave the cowboy a venomous look. "He's the problem," she said, pointing, "and I want him out of here."

Her name was Alice T. Ratchford; she was 28 years old and

132

worked in the cosmetics department of a local department store. No, she wasn't married, and the man on the couch was her boyfriend, Jackson Ford. They had been living together for the past eight months, but she had had enough.

Tonight he had accused her of all sorts of improprieties, and she wasn't about to take that kind of abuse from anyone. Ford was an insensitive, maniacally jealous oaf, who would probably break her into small pieces if we left without arresting him. She was ready and willing to sign complaints, swear out warrants, or do anything else to insure this menace to society was removed from the streets once and for all.

As she delivered this little diatribe, her voice kept inching up the scale and increasing in volume until she was screeching in a manner quite painful to the ears. She finally ran out of breath and flopped into an aluminum lawn chair by the door, one of the nicer pieces of furniture in the room.

The object of all this invective sat silently on the couch, a morose expression on his face. I hadn't even heard his side of the story yet, but I was already sympathizing with him. When quiet finally descended, Mr. Ford stirred and in a flat voice said, "Alice, I ain't never laid a finger on you, and I ain't about to start now. I got three people telling me you was out with Ray last night, and it ain't the first time." He looked at me. "She can sign all the warrants she wants, but I ain't done nothing to her, and she knows it."

Truth to tell, Miss Alice did not appear mishandled. Upset, yes, but injured, no. I have dealt with hundreds of battered women in my time, and they all had a certain wounded look in their eyes this one lacked.

I decided that she was not in any physical danger, but I wasn't sure I could say the same for Mr. Ford. As if on cue, Lady Alice leaped to her feet, fairly sizzling with rage. "Are you going to believe THAT son of a bitch?" she shrieked. "What have I got to do, let him kill me?"

I suppressed the urge to tell her that was an idea, since I much preferred investigating a nice, juicy murder to a pain-in-the-posterior family disturbance. Instead, I told her it was my opinion her life was not in mortal danger, and since there was no evidence of physical injury, I didn't think she had grounds to swear out a warrant.

"That's just the kind of answer I'd expect from a Goddamn man!" she screamed. "All you bastards stick together."

I was getting exceedingly tired of listening to her, so I turned to Mr. Ford, intending to give him some law enforcement advice concerning his part in this little play.

I never got the chance.

Before I could open my mouth, there was a shattering, clattering, crashing as something struck me a hard blow on the head and shoulders, knocking off my hat. I was engulfed by an object that pinned my arms and obscured my vision. I cried out in terror and began struggling wildly, trying to free myself.

I finally cast the thing from me. It skittered across the floor, bounced off the wall and came to a stop. It was a lawn chair. She had hit me with the lawn chair. I whirled around, trying to grab her, but she was already out the door and running down the sidewalk. By the time I got to the door, she had disappeared into the icy darkness. I fervently prayed she would die a lingering and painful death from quadruple pneumonia.

I went back inside, wondering why Lowery had not been able to stop her. In all the confusion I had not noticed him, but he should have been almost beside her. Why hadn't he at least blocked her escape? The answer was simple. He couldn't. He was presently lying on the floor, tears streaming down his face, shrieking with laughter. Good old Richard. My buddy. My backup. "Thanks for all your help," I said bitterly.

He rolled over on his back, knees pumping, hands clamped over his ears, gasping for breath. Even the taciturn Mr. Ford had to chuckle a little. "She gave you a right good lick with that chair, didn't she?"

I ignored him. Stepping over the helpless Lowery, I headed

for the door, already dreading what it was going to be like in the muster room when he finished describing my performance. As I went out the door, I heard him gasping to Ford, "Did you see...did you see...," Unable to continue, he lapsed into paroxysms of mirth once more.

29

WHY I HATE FAMILY DISTURBANCES

"109?"

I keyed the microphone, "Go ahead, I'm on Mobile Highway."

"10-4, 109, handle a family disturbance at apartment 24, Sutton Place Apartments." She paused a moment, then continued, "Back to 109. A neighbor called and said it sounded like they were really going at it."

"10-4, I'm enroute." Just what I needed. Another family disturbance. That would be my fourth tonight. The dispatcher called a backup for me, but unfortunately, I was only a few blocks away, while he was at the other end of the district. I swung my car around and headed for Sutton Place.

Family disturbance calls are cordially detested by most cops. For one thing, there is the real possibility that one or both of the combatants will turn on the interfering officer, and many cops have been injured or killed answering family fights. Third-party calls, like this one, are disliked more than any other.

Generally, those causing the disturbance are concentrating on being disagreeable with each other and tend to resent some spoil-sport cop barging in, quoting a bunch of laws. The way they express this resentment can range from elevating the cop's blood pressure to having his portrait, draped in black, hung in a place of honor at his department.

I have had my share of close calls and near misses while working family disturbances, and I haven't enjoyed them one bit. Now, I realize that having the mortal life scared out of you on frequent occasions is just the price of doing business when you are a cop. I understand this, but I don't enjoy being terrified. To me, it tends to diminish the enjoyment of law enforcement, and I am a firm believer that law enforcement should be fun as often as possible. This seems like a simple enough desire: more fun, less terror. But it doesn't always work out that way.

It usually comes down to the question of risk. In our job, we try to be as cautious as possible, but there are only so many precautions to be taken. Inevitably, there comes a time when a cop has to take the risks that go with the territory.

Walking up to a car after a night traffic stop is a good example. We hope to find nothing more lethal than a disgruntled taxpayer, a mouthy drunk, or a cocky teenager. The possibility that the driver is a homicidal psychotic, armed to the teeth, is in our minds, but we prefer not to dwell on it.

The same is true with family disturbances. We know a deranged killer with a sawed-off shotgun may be hiding behind the door, but that's life in the big leagues. If you can't stand the heat, get out of the kitchen, and all that.

This is not to imply that all family disturbance calls are life-or-death situations. Far from it. I have handled hundreds of family disturbance calls with no ill effects to anyone present. I have made arrests, been in some very tense situations, and done just fine. Some calls do stick in my mind, however, like the one at Sutton Place Apartments.

I got out of my car in front of the two-story building. The apartment I was seeking was on the second floor, so I trudged up the outside stairway, my equipment jingling and creaking.

The buildings were several different shades of red brick, and had wood trim painted a chestnut brown. White doors and a decorative steel railing on the second level gave it a neat and homey appearance. The rents were reasonable, and the tenants were mostly young working couples. As I started down the walkway, I heard yelling and screaming from the end apartment. Great, the battle was still going on. The door was standing open about four inches, and the hoarse tones of an obviously drunken male were being overridden by the shrill soprano of an enraged female.

It was a familiar chorus. ". . . and you don't give a damn about me or the baby. All you want to do is drink beer and . . ."

"Goddamnit, I love you, and I work my ass off 60 hours . . . "

"I want you out of my life and out of my apartment."

"Your apartment? Who the hell do you think pays the rent around here?"

What fun this was going to be. I pounded on the door. Instant silence. "Sheriff's department," I said loudly. "I need to talk with you." More silence. I waited a moment, then knocked again. "Sheriff's department, we've had a complaint from . . . "

That was as far as I got, because at that point the door was flung open, and the drunk came charging through like a fullback running for daylight.

It was at that instant I discovered I had made a tiny little mistake. You see, I should have been standing off to one side while I was beating on the door, in case someone was on the other side with a gun. This is one of those basic cop things we are taught in rookie school, and every eight-year-old learns from television. Unfortunately, I was just a tad careless, and, instead of standing to one side, I was standing directly in front of the door.

The drunk charged straight into me, carrying me backwards with his rush. I had only a brief impression of a very large man, wearing blue checkered pajama bottoms and nothing else. He had wild bloodshot eyes, shaggy hair, and two days' growth of beard. He was at least six inches taller and fifty pounds heavier than I was.

At the moment of collision, he grabbed me by the arms,

pinning them to my side, and we shot across the walkway and crashed into the railing. The force of the assault bent me backwards over the rail, and my straw Stetson spun away in the darkness. I was facing a massive, hairy chest, unable to move and rapidly approaching the outer limits of terror. From the iron grip on my arms, I could tell the guy was incredibly strong. One flick of those thick wrists, and I would sail over the rail to join my hat.

For some reason, he didn't toss me off the balcony. Instead, he stood me upright and screamed in my face, "PUT ME IN JAIL!"

Numb with fright, there was nothing in this world I wanted to do more, but he was going to have to let me go first. "Sir . . . " I began, but he cut me off.

"PUT ME IN JAIL, JUST PUT ME IN JAIL!" he shouted. To emphasize the point, he shook me until my teeth rattled.

I was desperately trying to inch my fingers down to my holster. If I could just get to my .38, jail wouldn't be necessary, but he had such a tight grip on me, I couldn't do it.

Even so, I was beginning to think I might live. Other than keeping me immobile, he had made no other offensive move. If only my backup would arrive. Cops are never around when you need them.

I tried to think of something I could say to quiet him. "Why do you want to go to jail?" I asked as calmly as possible.

"BECAUSE I'M A DRUNK," he shouted, giving me a shake with each word, "AND I BELONG IN JAIL!" Well, this made as much sense as anything else.

I finally did the first smart thing of the evening. Still completely helpless, I looked him in the eye and said sternly, "Okay, that's it. You're under arrest."

Immediately, a beatific smile lit up his face. "All riiiiight!" he said, releasing me abruptly. He turned and sprinted down the concrete walk, bare feet pounding.

Freed at last, I whipped out my gun and took off after him,

bellowing things like, "Okay, freeze, mister. Hold it right there! You better stop. I'm warning you; stop!" None of these had the slightest effect. He thundered down the stairs, crossed the parking lot, opened the back door of my cruiser, jumped in, and slammed it behind him.

By the time I arrived, chest heaving, streaming sweat, there was nothing more to do. I holstered my gun and stood, leaning against my car, trying to collect my shattered wits.

Tires crunched on the parking lot, and I looked up. My long-lost backup, David Hightower, had arrived. He pulled up beside me, "It looks like you've got it under control," he said cheerfully, not even bothering to get out.

I could only stare at him.

"Well, guess I'll get some coffee. Don't want to deprive those waitresses of their main thrill of the day." He drove off, and I spent a moment considering how his body would look riddled with bullets.

These reveries were interrupted by the guy in the back seat. "Hey!" he shouted.

I turned.

"Are we going to jail or what?"

"Yeah," I said, "we're going to jail."

He settled back in the seat contentedly. "Well, it's about damn time."

30

If You Say So

The woman was very angry. "Why are you stopping me?" she demanded, weaving slightly, the odor of alcohol unmistakable.

"Ma'am, you were all over the road, and you're driving with no headlights."

She glared at me. "Well, I can explain that."

"I'm all ears."

"I've been drinking all night, I'm very drunk, and I think I'm doing pretty well considering my condition!"

Oh.

31

TRAFFIC STOP #3

I was gaining on the little red sports car. With any luck, I would soon be close enough at least to get his tag number. I glanced at the speedometer. It was fluctuating between 70 and 80, plenty fast enough for the winding road we were on. We swung into another turn, and my cruiser drifted to the right. There were a series of jolting bumps as the right wheels ran off the pavement, and my heart jumped into my throat. I delicately brought the car back under control and returned to the pursuit.

That clinched it, this guy was guaranteed a ticket now.

I had been poking along a little side street off Fairfield Drive, minding my own business, enjoying the warm spring sunshine, when the little car flashed in front of me, well above the speed limit. I turned onto Fairfield Drive and accelerated.

I caught occasional glimpses of the red car when we hit a straightaway, but the driver wasn't acting like someone fleeing from the law. I doubted he even knew I was behind him. In the bright sunlight, it would have been almost impossible for him to notice my blue lights unless I was right on his bumper, and I was a long way from that.

I began to believe he was just enjoying a drive on a pretty afternoon, letting his nimble machine stretch out a bit. The problem was, this was not exactly a deserted road. We had already passed several cars, and at speeds close to 80, the slightest miscalculation on his part could lead to headlines and obituaries.

We came out of another turn, and I had closed the gap significantly. He was staying ahead of me on the turns, but I was gaining on the straights. I probably had twice the horsepower of his car and better acceleration at the top end.

I decided to take a calculated risk and try the siren. If he realized he was being pursued, he might decide to light the afterburner and take off in earnest. If he really made an effort to escape, he could probably do so easily, running away from me on the turns, then diving into a side street when he was out of sight.

On the other hand, if he was basically an honest citizen, albeit a reckless one, he wouldn't consider running, thinking he was well and truly caught. I hit the yelper and was gratified to see his head come up as he checked his mirror. There was a perceptible interval as we pounded down the road when I wondered if I had made a mistake. Finally, there was the reassuring glow of tail lights as he applied the brakes, and the little car, a red Triumph, I noted, slowed and coasted to a stop on the grass beside the road.

The driver was a tall reed of a man with a dashing handlebar mustache. He was wearing aviator sunglasses and a sporty leather cap. Both hands still on the steering wheel, he sat stiffly, looking straight ahead.

"May I see your driver's license, please?"

Silently, he took out his billfold, removed the license and handed it to me. I walked back to my cruiser to check for any outstanding warrants on William D. Stanley. There were none. I returned to his car and opened my citation book. Mr. Stanley had not moved a muscle.

I wrote him a citation for the speeding and probably could have added a charge of reckless driving as well, but I didn't think it would serve any useful purpose. The speeding ticket was going to cost him enough as it was.

"Mr. Stanley, I have charged you with doing 78 in a 45 mile per hour zone. You were probably above 80 several times, but I couldn't get close enough to know for sure."

He gave no sign he heard me, hands still clenched tightly on the wheel, still staring straight ahead.

I completed my explanations, and wordlessly, he signed the ticket. He placed his copy carefully in the glove box, put his hands back on the wheel, and lowered his forehead slowly until it was touching his hands. Then, very softly, he said, "Shit!"

It was the only word I heard him say.

32

The Dog That Didn't Bite

I have the greatest respect for dogs that don't know me. I have heard too many people when asked, "Does he bite?" laugh heartily and say, "Cream Puff bite? Well, he might lick you to death, but that would be about the worst he'd do."

Of course, these are the same people who stand around emergency rooms after Cream Puff has made a meal of a leg or a rump and say things like, "Gosh, he's never done that before." Well, as far as I'm concerned, any dog is capable of biting under the right circumstances.

While I've always been cautious around strange dogs, I am realistic about it. Just because there is a "Bad Dog" sign posted, doesn't mean the animal is a man-eater. Lots of people use the sign as a bluff or to protect them in the event of a law suit if Fido actually does take a chunk out of someone.

If I see a dog in a yard which has a warning sign posted, I'll rattle the gate or whistle. If the dog proceeds to hurl himself against the fence in a paroxysm of teeth-gnashing rage, I'll back off and wait for someone to come to the gate.

On the other hand, if the dog greets my presence with a yawn, or happily trots over to have his ears scratched, I'll ignore the sign and go into the yardand hope he doesn't have a big brother lurking in the bushes.

This strategy backfires occasionally, and there have been times I've set new records for the "Chain Link Fence Jump," but I have never been seriously bitten. So far.

Today things had been going well. I had gone to court, expecting to be tied up most of the day on an armed robbery case and discovered, to my joy, that the defendant had waited until the last minute to plead guilty. This was a double pleasure. Not only would I not have to spend the entire day sitting around the witness room waiting to testify, it meant we had convicted the guy on what we all felt was an extremely shaky case.

Everything hinged on the testimony of a disgruntled ex-girlfriend who had informed on her former lover after he dumped her. However, she was not exactly the most credible of witnesses, having a long history of narcotic and prostitution arrests. Additionally, she was suffering from pangs of conscience now that she realized she would be instrumental in sending him to prison. Luckily, the assistant state attorney worked out a deal with the public defender whereby the bad guy would agree to plead guilty to the crime and accept a ten-year sentence.

That was fine with me. He could have gotten life, but far better to settle for ten years and not have to sit around the courthouse all day.

Back on the street again, I answered a few routine calls, then stopped for a hamburger. I was just finishing lunch when I was sent to take a report of a stolen outboard motor. The dispatcher told me the homeowner would be coming from work, and if he was not there when I got to the house, I was to wait.

When I arrived at the house, the first thing I saw was a "Beware of the Dog" sign. The second thing I saw was a large white German shepherd resting in the shade of a bush, watching me watch him.

I went through my usual routine of banging the fence and whistling, but the dog didn't move. I unlatched the gate and stepped inside, carefully. Still no reaction from the dog. I proceeded slowly down the sidewalk, stepped up on the porch and rang the door bell. No one answered. There was a lawn chair on the porch, so I took a seat and began catching up on some paperwork. I glanced at the dog every now and then, but he had gone back to sleep.

A few minutes later, the complainant drove up. At the sound of the car, the dog bounded across the yard to greet his master, while I waited on the porch. He came down the walk, while the dog capered around him. I gave him my sincere smile. "Hi! did you call the about a stolen motor?"

"How did you get here?" he asked, ignoring my question.

I thought about this for a moment. "By car?" I replied tentatively.

"No, I mean, how did you get in the yard?"

"The gate wasn't locked, so I walked in."

"Thor didn't bother you?" he asked, gesturing toward the big shepherd.

"No, he ignored me."

He shook his head. "I don't understand it. He's bitten everyone, including my mother-in-law. I have to keep him chained up when strangers are around."

We went inside, and I took the report. He had stored the motor in his garage at the end of the summer, and discovered it was missing when he went to get it to go fishing. He was embarrassed to admit he had no idea how long it had been gone. "Don't worry about it;" I told him, "it happens all the time. You get so used to seeing something, you see it even when it's not there."

"My insurance company told me I would have to make a report before they would pay the claim, and I'm supposed to ask you for the complaint number."

I wrote it on the back of one of my business cards and handed it to him. He walked me to the front door and opened it. There was a tremendous crash as 110 pounds of enraged German shepherd smashed against the outside screen door. I yelped in terror and jumped back. "Down, Thor, down, boy!" the man shouted, "It's all right." The dog ignored him, trying his best to remove the door from the hinges.

He tried unsuccessfully for several minutes to calm his pet, but finally had to go outside and put the animal on a chain so I could leave. As I scuttled down the sidewalk, Thor nearly strangled himself trying to reach me. I drove off, happy I was still in one piece, Thor's thunderous barks speeding me on my way.

I still have no idea why he didn't have me for lunch when I first stepped through the gate.

33

JURY INSTRUCTIONS

The jury selection was proceeding slowly. The courtroom was filled with prospective jurors, attorneys, witnesses, defendants, off-duty cops, family members of victims and defendants, and a variety of staff personnel. I was not personally involved in any of the cases today; I was just the guard for the prisoners we had brought from the jail. They had been placed in the holding room, waiting to be called for their particular case.

I had finished the checking-in procedures, handed all the files to the clerk, made the required entries in the log book and was now standing outside the holding room, waiting for the first jury to be selected.

The assistant state attorney doing the questioning was fresh out of law school and had only recently joined the staff. A young eager beaver, he was reveling in his role as the hard-nosed but eloquent prosecutor, determined to right all the wrongs of society and see that the guilty were punished.

He was just finishing up his opening spiel to the prospective jurors and was really laying it on thick. Pacing back and forth, gesturing dramatically, his voice rising and falling like an evangelist, he had them all spellbound. The jurors, that is. The rest of us, those of us who had been through this a hundred times, were not so spellbound. In fact, most of us were wishing young

Clarence Darrow would hurry up and finish.

Spectators talked quietly, clerks and secretaries carrying files hurried in and out of the courtroom, attorneys waiting for their cases to be called held whispered conferences with their clients, and high above it all, in lofty isolation, the judge rocked slowly in his chair, viewing the proceedings through half-closed eyes, watching the wheels of justice grind ponderously forward.

". . . and all of you know that in our great country our system of justice is founded on the Constitution?" the young prosecutor said.

The men and women all nodded solemnly.

"And all of you know that, as citizens of the United States of America, we all have certain rights that are guaranteed by the Constitution?"

They nodded again.

"And all of you know that, under our system of justice, all people accused of any crime are considered guilty until proven innocent?"

Their heads bobbed up and down in unison.

He continued his remarks, but I was no longer listening. For me, time was suspended. I looked around the room, but everything seemed as it was. The same conversations were going on, the same clerical people moved back and forth, the judge still rocked in his chair, but something was wrong. I was sure I had just heard the prosecutor state that under our system of justice all people were guilty until proven innocent. Not only that, but the prospective jurors had agreed with him. Every single one of them. I was sure it was just a slip of the tongue, but he had said it, nevertheless, which meant he might have introduced a reversible error.

Actually, I didn't know for sure, not being a judge. Truth to tell, I wasn't even sure I had heard him say what I thought I had heard him say.

The prosecutor had completed his soliloquy with a ringing declaration that justice be done and then taken his seat. The assistant public defender was walking towards the jurors, preparing to begin his own statement, oblivious to the error made by his opponent. I looked around, wondering if I was the only person who had heard the prosecutor's mistake.

An attorney I knew was walking toward the prosecutors' table, a broad smile on his face. He bent down and spoke to the senior of the group, who listened a moment, then motioned the young prosecutor over. They held a whispered conference, and I saw the young man pale. The group of prosecutors approached the judge, the eager beaver looking like a man about to receive the death sentence. They talked with the judge a moment, and he smiled slightly. The public defender was droning on about fair and impartial verdicts and guilt beyond a reasonable doubt, when the judge interrupted him. He asked the stenographer to read back the prosecutor's last instruction to the jurors.

She went through her tapes until she found his statements. In a clear voice she read, "And all of you know that under our system of justice anyone accused of a crime is guilty until proven innocent."

The room echoed with laughter while the young prosecutor turned several interesting shades of red. The only people who did not laugh were the jurors, who really did not understand what was going on. To his absolute mortification, the poor guy had to step back in front of them and correct his mistake, asking them if they understood that under our system of justice accused criminals were actually innocent until proven guilty and not guilty until proven innocent as he had told them at first.

They nodded just as enthusiastically as before.

34

ATTEMPTED BRIBERY

". . . and this is the outside speaker switch," I said, completing the little tour of the inside of my cruiser.

Grady Ackerman nodded, obviously impressed. He gestured toward the profusion of knobs, switches, and buttons scattered across the dashboard that operated the siren, blue lights, radio, and outside speaker. "Do you ever push the wrong button?"

I laughed, "It happens all the time. I'll get in a chase and try to do eight things at the same time. I've yelled at someone, over the outside speaker, to get out of the way, then discovered I was using the radio microphone."

"I'll bet that woke up some dispatchers," he chuckled. Eyes bright with interest, he watched my every move as I put the car in gear and turned onto the highway, ready to combat a little crime. He was reveling in the experience of riding with a deputy sheriff.

I had met Grady only the day before. He lived in an older residential section of concrete block houses on generous, tree-shaded lots. Although the houses were relatively small, the owners took great pride in their appearance and the yards were immaculate. It was not a troublesome area, and calls were few. I had been dispatched to his home to take a report of a stolen bike.

Although it seemed minor enough, I wasn't looking forward

to taking the call. I had learned through experience that these calls can be surprisingly unpleasant. There is something about stealing from a child that enrages many people, particularly the parents of the child.

Not infrequently, an irritated parent uses the opportunity to deliver a heated lecture about the lack of law enforcement in his neighborhood, the failings of the criminal justice system, and the woeful decline in the quality of law enforcement officers in general. Not surprisingly, some of my shorter-tempered brethren have taken exception to these kinds of comments, and arrests have even occurred. So perhaps I can be forgiven for being a little wary as I pulled into the driveway of the neat house belonging to the Ackermans.

I need not have worried. Grady Ackerman was a cheerful, friendly guy, only a few years older than me, looking very much the federal civil servant he was. With his short hair and all-American looks, he could easily have passed for a cop himself. "Did you call the sheriff's department?" I asked.

He smiled ruefully, "Sure did. Someone stole my boy's bike right out of the front yard." He opened the door. "Come in."

I stepped into a small but spotless living room. An attractive redhead joined us, and Ackerman introduced me to his wife, Elaine. "Do you think you can find Jason's bike?" she asked.

"Well, I'm going to try," I said in what I hoped was an optimistic tone. Actually, I wasn't too hopeful. The hard-working little bike thieves who lived close by would quickly strip the useable parts and either re-paint the frame or discard it.

About the only way we would get this bike back would be to find it abandoned someplace or actually catch someone riding it. Neither possibility rated very high in the laws of probability, as far as I was concerned.

As I was taking the information, a very dejected Jason arrived. He had been out walking the neighborhood, looking for the missing bike without success. He gave me a minute description of his beloved two-wheeler which I wrote carefully on the report.

I did what I could to cheer him up, but I didn't make much progress until I offered to let him get inside my cruiser. He brightened immediately, "Can I blow the siren?"

I considered the possibility of outraged neighbors complaining about the noise, but what the hell. Even the sheriff might understand. "Sure you can blow the siren."

"OH BOY!" Jason shouted, almost tearing the screen door off in his rush to get outside. His mom and dad followed us out to the car, where I let young Jason turn on the blue lights, swivel the spotlight and give a satisfying shriek with the siren.

Through it all, I noticed that Grady was as fascinated as his son. I accepted Mrs. Ackerman's offer of a cup of coffee, mainly because I had a proposition I wanted to make to Grady.

When we were sipping our coffee, I turned to him, "Would you be interested in riding with me as an observer?" There was a flash of eagerness in his eyes, quickly masked by an elaborate disinterest. "Well, I don't know," he said doubtfully. "What would it involve?"

"Well, you would ride around with me, watching while I answered calls and made arrests. You'd learn more about law enforcement in eight hours than from a lifetime of television watching."

He didn't seem too eager, and I was surprised at his reluctance. I thought he'd jump at the chance.

Then I saw him glance at his wife, and I realized his problem. Elaine was scared to death. With only TV as reference, she probably had visions of hubby being riddled with bullets in a shootout, or stabbed to death by some maniac. She had no way of knowing how boring patrol work could be or the endless tedium of a slow shift.

Once I realized her unspoken fears, I shifted quickly into reassurance mode. "Let me assure you," I said to her, "there is very little risk involved. We'll be spending most of our time chasing speeders, looking for lost pets, and, of course, taking reports of stolen bikes." They laughed. "I'm afraid it won't be as exciting as you might hope,'' I concluded.

Elaine looked much relieved at my recital, and Grady perked up considerably when it became apparent he might get his chance. I was proud of my smooth performance. It was essentially true, but of course, there was no way of predicting what might happen.

We decided he could ride the following night, on the afternoon shift. I would pick him up at his house after getting permission from the shift commander, but that was only a formality.

At 3:30 the next afternoon, I turned into the Ackerman driveway, and the whole family was waiting to greet me. Elaine took several snapshots of Grady and me standing beside my cruiser while an almost out-of-his-mind Jason ran around screaming, ''My dad's going to be a cop, my dad's going to be a cop!''

We loaded up and, with Elaine and Jason waving, set out to fight crime. It reminded me of a leave-taking of a soldier going off to war. I hoped the analogy wouldn't go any farther than the leave-taking part.

The first few hours passed rapidly. I made a few more traffic stops than usual, primarily for Grady's benefit; investigated a report of a vandalism to a church, three BB holes through a stained glass window; arrested a shoplifter at a department store; mediated a dispute between two sisters arguing over a stereo that had belonged to their deceased mother; directed traffic around a wreck; and took two coffee breaks.

Grady was good company. As a computer systems analyst, he had a job with very little real excitement. It paid the bills, but like most men, he had a secret hankering to take a few risks now and then. Riding around with a cop was a perfect outlet for that desire.

I answered his questions as well as I could and filled him full of war stories. Even though I had been a deputy sheriff for barely a year, I quickly fell into the role of the grizzled law enforcement veteran.

As we patrolled the streets, I pointed out the street walkers, indicating the ones I knew to be female impersonators; I mentioned various spectacular incidents like armed robberies and murders at now-calm locations; and showed him some of the local hoodlums I knew who had rather lurid records. He was enthralled.

It was just after dark when we were dispatched to the Sunset Motel to investigate a report of an unknown disturbance.

The Sunset was fairly notorious. It had been built during the 1940's, and each "room" was a separate cottage. Now a shabby, crumbling relic of a bygone era, it was frequented by a fairly rough crowd: whores with their tricks, boozers looking for some place cheap to have a bender, and dopers wanting a place to crash. It was strictly cash-up-front, and no checks or credit cards.

As we pulled into the driveway, we met a battered Oldsmobile with one headlight. There were six grubby-looking guys inside, and I had a gut feeling they were the source of the disturbance. I turned on the blue lights and pulled in front of the car. Grady got out and stood by the passenger side of the cruiser, as I had instructed him to do. Although he was unarmed, they wouldn't know that, and with his coat and tie, he looked exactly like a plainclothes cop.

Six pairs of nervous eyes watched me approach their car. "Driver's license, please," I said to the driver. While he fished it out of his tattered jeans, I used the opportunity to shine my flashlight around the inside of the car. All six occupants were thoroughly disreputable-looking, with various combinations of beards, long, shaggy hair, and psychedelic clothing.

I looked at the driver, and he shifted his eyes uneasily. "Your left headlight is out," I said. He stared at me blankly, and I added, "And we got a report of some kind of disturbance here. Would you know anything about that?"

He licked his lips, "We had an argument, and it got a little loud, that's all."

I collected identification from everyone and walked back to my cruiser. As I was reaching for the microphone to check warrants on the names, a fat, owlish-looking man came waddling across the courtyard, his thick glasses reflecting the blue lights. "I want them out of here," he said in a high, thin voice. "I asked them to stop all that yelling, and they cursed me." He wiped drops of sweat off his face, "They've been here for two days, and they're nothing but trouble."

"I take it you're the manager?"

He bent down to look in the window, his eyes magnified by the lenses. He was rapidly losing his hair on top but had artfully arranged the few surviving strands in such a manner that the maximum amount of bare scalp was covered. It was an impressive, though ludicrous, effort. "Yes, I'm the manager," he huffed.

"They'll be on their way in a few minutes," I said reassuringly, "just as soon as I know if any of them are wanted for anything."

I ran all the names, and in a few minutes, the dispatcher came back, "109?"

"Go ahead."

"We may have a hit."

I pulled the door closed and keyed the microphone again. "Go ahead."

"We have a VOP (Violation Of Probation) and an FTA (Failure To Appear) from circuit court on Allison James Meadows; no bond on the VOP."

This sounded promising. "10-4, I'll be out of the car a minute."

Grady hadn't really understood what was going on, but he knew something was up. I said, "We've got some warrants on Meadows," I said. "He's the one in the middle in the back seat. You stand by the left side of their car and be ready to go either way, in case he tries to run." Grady nodded, his eyes wide.

When he was in position, I said, "Mr. Meadows, step out of the car, please." I took a step back and placed my hand on the butt of my revolver in a rather ostentatious manner, just so they would get the idea. After some hesitation, Meadows slowly worked his way across the legs of his companions and stepped from the car.

He was very small, perhaps 5′ 4″, and couldn't have weighed more than 100 pounds. "Hands on top of the car, please, feet back and spread 'em." He "assumed the position," as we say in the biz, and I patted him down for weapons, then cuffed his hands behind him. I turned him around. "We have a warrant for your arrest on a violation of probation."

I got a better look at him in the glare from my headlights. He had long, ginger-colored hair and a matching beard, and the bluest eyes I have ever seen on a man. If his face hadn't been so gaunt, he would have been quite handsome. He stared at me, and those blue eyes had a flat, lifeless quality I found disconcerting. "You're making a mistake," he said.

"That may be true," I said, as I led him toward my cruiser, "and if I am, you'll be released with my apologies." He offered no resistance as I loaded him in the cage.

The motel manager approached timidly. He leaned over and whispered, "Will you tell these other people to leave?" Little rivulets of sweat were coursing down his face, and he twisted his pudgy hands nervously. "I don't want any trouble from his friends."

"I don't think they are going to stick around now that we have arrested this one," I said, nodding at Meadows.

Sure enough, as soon as I returned the various ID's, they drove off without a word, scarcely glancing at their comrade.

We headed toward the jail, and Meadows was silent in the back seat, staring glumly out the window. I was pleased with the capture. Stumbling on a wanted fugitive didn't happen very often, and this would make Grady's night even more memorable.

We talked about how warrants were filed and the meaning of a violation of probation and failure to appear. There was a momentary lull in the conversation, and from the back seat Meadows said calmly, "I'll give you each a $1,000 if you'll let me go."

I almost drove off the road. "Thanks for the offer, Meadows, but we don't take checks." I tried to sound light-hearted, but I was definitely startled.

"I've got the money," he said. "Let me make one phone call, and I'll have it here in ten minutes."

Grady was slack-jawed with astonishment. This was turning out to be a memorable night, all right. "No, thanks, Allison, I don't like to take bribes; it makes it hard for me to sleep at night."

His empty eyes bored through me. "$5,000 for each of you." He thought Grady was a cop.

This had gone far enough. "Meadows, if you say another word about offering us money I'm going to charge you with attempted bribery."

Allison was silent for the rest of the journey to the jail. I booked him on the warrants, but we didn't speak of his attempted bribe. Back on patrol once more, Grady asked, "Why didn't you charge him with attempted bribery?"

I sighed. "Because it's a tough case to prove. It would have come down to his word against ours, and we might not have gotten a conviction." I didn't add that Grady would probably find himself caught up in an endless round of depositions, suppression hearings, and trials. Since we had the two solid warrants against him, I couldn't see much point in trying to pursue the bribery charge.

"Do you think he could have come up with the $10,000?" Grady asked.

I had considered this. "It's possible," I said, "I'm sure he's a dope dealer."

Grady shook his head. "Well, I guess you're used to that sort of thing in your job; it probably happens all the time."

"Oh, yeah, all the time," I agreed. I didn't have the heart to tell him that was the first time anyone had ever offered me a bribe. As it turned out, no one has offered since.

YOU'RE UNDER ARREST

Allison Meadows was indeed a drug dealer and a drug addict, too. He served some time for his probation violation and was released. About three years after he attempted to bribe me, he was found dead of a heroin overdose in another sleazy motel, not far from the Sunset.

35

NIGHT VISITOR

It had been a busy midnight shift, but things finally began to slow down around 4:00 A.M. I had reports to do, so I pulled into a parking lot behind a shopping center to write for a while. On my left was a large open area about the size of a football field. The site of a future construction project, it was gradually being filled in, and there were dozens of piles of dirt and rubble scattered around.

I finished one report and was well into another when a flash of movement caught my eye. I studied the darkened field for a few minutes but saw nothing suspicious, so I began writing again.

A few moments later it happened again. Something moved out there in the darkness, and I snapped my head around. Nothing. I scanned every inch of the field, but I couldn't see anything to account for the movement. Again, I went back to the reports. Again, something moved. Again, I tried to spot the cause. Again, I failed.

Enough was enough. Something was going on out there, and I was going to find out what it was. I switched on the spotlight and played it over the dirt piles. In the beam of the spotlight I finally saw something tangible. Several small, dark shapes scuttled out of the light. Rats. The field was full of them, but they were invisible in the darkness, and I could not have seen them without the spotlight.

I suspected that someone was hiding behind the dirt piles and popping his head up every so often to see where I was. Finding him in the dark would be difficult, because I certainly couldn't drive through the field. On the other hand, I would see anyone who tried to leave. I turned off the spotlight and sat quietly, letting my eyes adjust to the darkness.

Five minutes later, I finally saw it.

Dropping silently out of the darkness above the field, an enormous barn owl dipped and soared among the dirt piles, its pale wings flashing in the moonlight. A moment later, the owl rose into the air, the limp form of a dead rat dangling from one talon.

I couldn't believe it. In the midst of urban sprawl, this magnificent predator was out here in the dark catching its supper, oblivious to the occasional cars and trucks going by, ignoring my cruiser less than a hundred feet away. I felt like Marlin Perkins on "Wild Kingdom."

I had to tell someone about this amazing experience. Excitedly, I called the deputy who was working the district next to mine and asked him to meet me in the parking lot. When he pulled up, I described the sudden appearance of the big owl and the primal beauty of it as it went about its task of capturing a meal. He listened politely, but I could tell he wasn't too impressed. "I guess you really had to be here," I concluded, a little lamely. He nodded and started to speak, when the owl swooped down again. "Look, look," I hissed. We watched as the bird repeated his performance, taking another rat and disappearing into the darkness.

Almost overcome with the sheer rapture of it all, I turned to my companion. "Wasn't that something?"

He had a wistful expression, and I was touched. The boy was basically a redneck and not someone who I thought would be impressed by the wonders of nature, but maybe I was wrong.

He sighed and shook his head. "I knew I should have brought my shotgun tonight. I believe I could have dropped him from here. "He sighed again. "That sucker sure would have looked fine over my fireplace."

36

YOU'RE UNDER ARREST —
I'M NOT KIDDING

The restaurant was packed when we arrived, and we had to wait 30 minutes before we were seated. I would not have chosen this particular place, because it was always jammed in the evenings, but I had not picked it. With my wife out of town for a week, some friends had invited me to accompany them for dinner.

I had known JackiAnn and her husband, Steven, for 15 years. Steve was one of the few life insurance agents I could stand to be around for more than ten minutes. Quiet but friendly, he had a good sense of humor, and I enjoyed his company.

JackiAnn, on the other hand, was a nonstop talker who had opinions about everything and everyone and felt duty bound to share them with anyone within earshot. She was relentlessly nosey and enjoyed interrupting conversations she was not even a part of, demanding to know who was being discussed. Although I frequently found her irritating, I had learned to keep my cool. . . most of the time. She was a small, intense, dark-haired woman with quick brown eyes. Although pretty, her abrupt manner and abrasive inquisitiveness turned me off.

As we waited, she rattled on and on about how she just loved coming here because of the authentic atmosphere. It had atmosphere, all right, but the wall-to-wall crowds made it hard to appreciate.

It was 15 minutes before a harried young waiter came jogging up, said his name was Eric, and announced it would be his pleasure to serve us. We gave him our drink orders and he disappeared into the maelstrom.

JackiAnn asked me about a recent, well-publicized murder and demanded to know why we had not arrested the perpetrator. The case involved an elderly widow who had been found in her apartment raped and strangled. I could tell JackiAnn was not impressed with our efforts, but it's always difficult to explain to non-cops why some crimes are much harder to solve than others.

I was trying to tell her we didn't have any decent leads, when I was interrupted by the arrival of Eric with our drinks. I turned to take my beer and was startled when he suddenly threw the tray of drinks over my shoulder; then fell in my lap. The drinks crashed to the floor, splashing JackiAnn, who shrieked with fright. It took a moment for Eric and me to untangle ourselves, but I realized he had not jumped into my lap on purpose; he had been shoved.

A drunk had been sleeping at the bar, and when one of the employees tried to awaken him, the drunk lashed out with one arm, propelling the guy into Eric, who ended up in my lap. I saw that the cause of all this excitement was a skinny kid who couldn't have weighed 140 pounds. He was now fully awake and arguing with the bartender. Waiters were beginning to converge, and it looked as though the situation was well in hand. I didn't think they would have any trouble with him.

A waiter was trying to ease the guy toward the door. He took a few steps, then jerked away. "Leave me alone," he shouted. There was instant silence in the bar except for the beeping and blooping of a video game in the corner.

In the midst of this sound void, JackiAnn yelled, "You're a cop, Don; do something!"

Every head in the place swung toward me, and I devoutly

wished I had my .38; I would have shot her dead. I had to get involved now, but it wasn't something I was eager to do. Out of uniform and dressed for a fun night on the town, I could hardly have looked less like a cop.

I shuffled across the floor, silently cursing her. The only one who wasn't looking at me was the drunk. I tapped him on the shoulder. "Excuse me, friend, but I think you're going to have to leave."

He swung around, swaying alarmingly. "You the manager?" he demanded, glaring at me.

"No, I'm a deputy sheriff."

He surveyed my casual attire, and his lip curled in contempt. "You ain't no Deputy."

There were a few chuckles from the crowd, and my cheeks flamed. "Oh, yes, I am," I said, flashing my badge.

He tried to focus, almost falling over from the effort. I steadied him, and he straightened up. "Nah, you're no cop. I know 'em all. I never heard of you."

"Maybe not," I said, irritated, "but I am a cop, and you are going to leave."

He extended both arms in a dramatic gesture. "Okay, if you're a cop, arrest me, put the cuffs on me."

"Look, I'm off duty, and I don't want to arrest you; I just want to eat my dinner."

"Arrest me," he demanded, waving his arms in my face.

Someone shouted, "Oh, go ahead and arrest him."

I sighed. "I told you, I'm off duty. I don't have handcuffs."

"I knew it," he crowed, "You ain't no cop. He turned back to the bartender. "Give me another beer."

"I'm not going to argue with you, sport; I am a deputy, and you are going to leave."

He flicked a hand at me. "Shoo, fly, ya bother me." The crowd roared.

I felt my temper begin to go. I took him firmly by one arm, pulled him away from the bar and steered him toward the door, as the crowd booed. Once outside, he wasn't so cocky. One of the waiters had accompanied me, and I felt a lot more confident with the odds clearly in my favor.

We stopped, and he tried to pull away. "Get your hands off me; I ain't done nothing."

"That's not exactly true. You've already done more than enough to be arrested, and I suggest you leave peacefully; I'll be happy to call a cab for you."

"I ain't leaving," he said belligerently, "I still got a beer left."

"If you don't leave, I'll have to arrest you."

He snorted, "You ain't no cop."

"Look, we've already been through this. I am a deputy; you are going to leave, or I am going to arrest you."

"I ain't going!" he shouted.

"Fine," I shouted back, "then you're under arrest." I turned to one of the waiters. "Call the police, and ask them to send an officer to transport this guy to jail for me." Since we were within the city limits, I would have to depend on the assistance of the Pensacola Police Department.

The waiter went inside, and the drunk spun away from me and lurched across the parking lot. I chased him down, and he struggled to free himself. "Turn me loose; I'll leave."

"It's too late now, friend; you're under arrest."

"No, I'm not."

"Yes, you are."

"I'm not under arrest; I ain't done nothing."

"You are under arrest, I'm not kidding, so you might as well calm down."

"You ain't no cop, let me go." He struggled harder, and I had to use both hands to restrain him. "Help, police!" he wailed.

Attracted by his cries, two men approached us. "What's going on?" a paunchy guy with cowboy boots and a western shirt asked.

"I'm an off-duty deputy," I panted, trying to grab the kid's flailing arms, "I've arrested this guy, and I'm waiting for a cruiser car to take him to jail for me."

"He ain't no cop," the drunk yelled, "he's trying to rob me."

Cowboy's companion, a weasely little redneck with a scraggly mustache and no chin, decided to get involved. "You really a cop?"

"Yes, I'm a cop," I gasped, "I've got my badge in my back pocket, but I've kind of got my hands full right this minute or I'd show it to you." Neither man made a move to help me, but I finally pinned the kid against a car and extracted the badge case. The two men examined it carefully while the drunk continued to yell for the police, drawing more people to the scene.

A fiftyish woman with neon-yellow hair and brown lipstick stepped foward. "Why are you hurting that young man?"

"Lady, this guy's under arrest, and the cops are on the way."

She regarded me suspiciously, "You a policeman?"

"I'm a deputy sheriff." I nodded toward the overweight cowboy. "Take a look for yourself." She joined the little group huddled around my badge case.

Finally, after several eons, a city police cruiser turned into the driveway and pulled up beside us, and a cop I didn't recognize got out of the car. From the razor-sharp creases in his pants, the gleam of his collar brass, and his earnest, youthful appearance, I knew he had to be a rookie. Although exhausted, I managed to force a smile. "Boy, am I glad to see you."

He didn't return the smile. "What's the problem?"

The weasel pointed to me. "This guy says he's a cop."

"He ain't no cop," the drunk yelled, renewing his efforts to free himself, "He's trying to rob me."

"I'm Don Parker, and I'm with the sheriff's department."

"Do you have some identification, Mr. Barker?"

"It's 'Parker', and yes, I have identification."

Someone handed him my badge case, and he examined it minutely. "You a full-time deputy?"

"Yes, I'm a full-time deputy," I said, irritated, "Are you a full-time policeman?" He ignored the sarcasm, as my prisoner continued to wail.

YOU'RE UNDER ARREST — I'M NOT KIDDING

Eventually, the cop came to the conclusion I was, in fact, a real deputy sheriff, and he agreed to transport the drunk to jail, with the understanding I would meet him there to do the booking. He and my still-wailing prisoner drove off, and the crowd drifted away.

I went back inside and found my friends just finishing their meals. I was hot, sweaty, hungry, and irritated. Naturally, JackiAnn started in on me. "Well, did you arrest the guy?"

"No, I gave him dancing lessons."

"Oh, aren't we the grouchy one."

I glared at her. "I wouldn't have gotten involved if you hadn't started yelling."

"Well, you're the cop. Aren't you supposed to enforce the law?"

"For crying out loud, JackiAnn, I'm off duty, out of uniform, in a restaurant, trying to relax. They didn't need me; they're used to handling drunks."

"Well, pardon me for living."

Steve agreed to drop me off at the jail so I could take care of the paperwork. It was a quiet trip. JackiAnn pouted the whole way, since she wasn't able to order the Double Chocolate Whammy dessert. I was grateful for the silence.

37

HOW TO SOLVE A PROBLEM

"I ain't going any damn where's!" The enormous drunk glared at us, weaving back and forth, reeking of beer. The ragged T-shirt he wore barely covered his thickly muscled torso, and I stared, fascinated, as the sinews in his arms corded and flexed as he moved. I could imagine only too well what it would be like to fight someone that big inside this small room. I glanced at the lieutenant. He looked as worried as I felt. "Mr. Jackson," he said, and the drunk turned. "We're just trying to solve this problem, and one way to do that would be for you to leave for a while to let things cool off."

"I ain't got no problem!" Jackson bellowed. "My old lady, she got a problem, but I ain't got no problem, and I ain't leaving my own house, and I ain't going to jail."

"No one said anything about going to jail," the lieutenant said soothingly. "You haven't done anything to be arrested for." Jackson raised a fist that looked like a cinder block. "Well, maybe I'll do something."

I had been edging around behind him as he talked, and with these words, I put down my notebook and took a firm grip on my heavy flashlight. I had a feeling I was going to need it in just a second or two.

I knew the call was going to be trouble as soon as I got it, a few minutes before quitting time, at the end of a really nasty day shift. Although assigned to me, it sounded serious enough for the dispatchers to take the extraordinary step of asking the shift commander if he could back me up, since no one else was available.

We arrived together and found a woman and two kids being consoled by neighbors in the front yard. "He's drunk again, and I can't stand anymore," she wailed. "You've got to do something, or he's going to kill me."

"Ma'am, we'll do what we can," I told her. "Are you willing to sign a warrant against him?"

She rolled her eyes fearfully, "The last time I did that, he broke my jaw."

"He's been arrested before?" the lieutenant asked.

"Oh, yeah," she said. "He just got out for beating up two city cops at a bar downtown." My mouth went dry. Why, oh, why hadn't I listened to my mother and become an accountant?

"We'll talk to him and see if we can work something out," I said. We headed up the sidewalk, and that was when I noticed the screen door. Actually there wasn't all that much to see. It was a crumpled wreck, dangling from one hinge, splintered and torn as though a rhinoceros had charged through it. I was not comforted at the analogy.

"Please be careful," the woman said as we approached the door, effectively destroying my last shred of confidence.

We looked through the open door and saw The Incredible Hulk sitting on the couch, surrounded by empty beer cans. I rapped on the door frame with my flashlight, and he looked up. "Whadda ya want?" he growled.

"Can we talk with you a moment, Mr. Jackson?" I asked, trying to sound friendly and non-threatening. I really wanted him to like me.

He stared at us for a long moment and finally said, "Well, come on in." We went inside and attempted to discuss his marital problems, but we didn't make much headway. Now we were at what I regarded as the crucial point in our negotiations.

My flashlight was at the ready, but I was not confident I was going to survive the next few minutes. I hoped I wouldn't have to shoot him. That might really make him mad.

"Mr. Jackson, there's no reason to fight," my lieutenant told him. "We know you don't want to cause anyone any trouble." Like hell he didn't, but I was rooting for the lieutenant. Jackson slowly lowered his fist but continued to glare at him. "You can't put me out of my own house."

"We don't want to put you out of your house," the boss said. "We just want you to go someplace for a few hours and cool off."

"Yeah," I chimed in, "can't you go get a beer someplace?"

Jackson thought this over, then began shaking his head. "I ain't got no money."

I looked at those massive arms and an idea began to form in my mind. "Look, Mr. Jackson, if you'll agree to leave, I'll personally give you a ride, and I think the lieutenant and I can give you a few bucks." Jackson looked interested, and I thought quickly, "The department maintains a special emergency fund for deserving people, and I think you'll qualify."

"You think so?"

"I'm sure of it. Of course, you'll have to sign a special voucher."

"Oh, sure," he said eagerly, "I'll sign."

I leafed through my notebook until I found a missing person report. "Sign on the line where it says 'parent or guardian'." He scrawled his name unsteadily. The lieutenant and I managed to come up with four dollars between us, and I handed it to Mr. Jackson.

We left the house together, Jackson smiling, the lieutenant and I relieved. As he got into my cruiser, his wife approached, looking worried. "Are you going to put him in jail?"

"No, ma'am, your husband is going to leave for a few hours until he's in a better mood. Right, Mr. Jackson?"

"Damn right," Jackson said enthusiastically. "I'll be back after a while, honey."

She smiled uncertainly but seemed agreeable. We drove away, and I dropped him at the front door of a nearby bar. I glanced at my watch. There was still 20 minutes until the next shift came on. "Mr. Jackson, if you go back to your house before 4:00, the deal's off and you have to give the money back."

He nodded solemnly, "Don't worry, I'll be right here." He staggered into the bar, and I drove off, satisfied I had successfully solved another law enforcement problem.

38

ARMED ROBBERY

Many law enforcement officers become heroes by simply being in the right place at the right time and reacting properly to the circumstances which arise while they are at that place at that time. Sound confusing? I'll try to make it clearer by relating the story of the armed robbery that occurred while I was reading a magazine at Carver's Drug Store.

Carver's was one of my favorite hangouts. Long gone now, it was one of those neighborhood pharmacies most of us grew up with. Concentrating on prescriptions and medical supplies, it had one of the few authentic soda fountains left in Pensacola. The food was nutritious and reasonably priced, and the service slow but friendly. I liked to eat lunch there on my days off, and afterwards I would wander over to the magazine rack and browse a while.

The day of the armed robbery, I had just finished one of their tasty club sandwiches, a slice of cherry pie, and several cups of coffee. Pleasantly full, I was soon engrossed in the magazines. I heard the bell tinkle on the front door behind me. I looked around and saw a thin black man step up to the counter. Our eyes met, but I quickly looked away. I didn't feel like talking to anyone; I just wantea to read my magazine.

He spoke to the woman at the cash register, but his voice was too low to catch the words. The register opened and a paper bag crackled. A few seconds later, the bell sounded on the front door, and I was alone again.

A few minutes later, I finally picked out a magazine and headed for the check-out counter. I reached for my wallet, and as I did, I felt the butt of my revolver jab me in the ribs. Like most cops, I am always armed when off duty.

I put the magazine on the counter and placed a few bills on top of it. The elderly woman at the register looked pale and shaken, but I didn't think too much of it. She was always complaining about her digestion, and I was always sympathetic.

"How are you today?" I asked, prepared for a litany of symptoms. She didn't move, and I noticed the cash register was open but there was no money in the drawer. I frowned. Something was wrong here. "I see you have no money," I said, pointing to the register.

She looked at the drawer and slowly began to shake her head. "How are you going to make change?" I asked.

"Change?"

"Yes, for my magazine. You owe me 46 cents." She looked at me, and I was suddenly aware that tears were running down her cheeks. She put her hands to her face and began to sob. I was horrified. "Hey, it's all right. I don't need the change that bad; you keep it."

While this little drama was going on, I had been aware of the wail of an approaching siren growing louder by the second. Tires squealed in the parking lot, and the siren ended in mid-wail. Deputy Dale Krause, revolver in hand, came running into the store. He looked around quickly and spotted me. "Where did he go?" he asked urgently.

"Who?"

"The robber."

I stared at him. "What robber?"

Dale was confused. "The one who just robbed this store."

"This store? No one has robbed this store."

The sobbing woman pointed. "He ran out the door. A black man, tall and thin. He had a gun."

I almost passed out. The guy had robbed the place while I was less than twenty feet away. Dale holstered his gun. "You didn't see anything?"

I was in shock. I shook my head, "No, I was standing by the magazine rack. I saw the guy come in, but I had my back turned. I didn't even know he had done it."

A smile tugged at the corners of Dale's mouth, but he suppressed it and opened his notebook. While he talked to the woman, I wandered toward the back of the store. My stomach churned. I had witnessed an armed robbery and didn't even know it. Of course, if I had tried to do something I might well be dead now, so I guess I was lucky. It was small comfort.

Dale joined me after a few minutes and took what information I could give him. It wasn't much. After we finished the paperwork, I turned to him. "Say, Dale, you're not going to tell anyone about this, are you?"

He was shocked. "Tell anyone? Why would I do that? I know how embarrassing that could be for you. He gave me a big wink and put his finger across his lip. It's our little secret. Mum's the word."

I was sure he wouldn't tell a soul. And he didn't . . . unless you count every deputy east of the Mississippi.

39

A CLEAN SHOOTING

I glanced at my watch: 12:10 A.M. That made it December 17, 1977, my brother Roger's birthday. I debated going back inside and calling him to sing, Happy Birthday, over the phone. The thought of waking him up was a pleasing one, but so was the thought of getting home. The urge to go home won out over the urge to harass my brother.

It was a cool night with a thick blanket of fog shrouding the buildings around the jail. The street lights were dim pinpoints in the grey night, and the county hospital, only a few hundred feet away, was invisible.

I got in the car and turned on the wipers as soon as I cranked up. I let the defroster struggle with the mist on the windshield and then scrubbed at it with my fingers, opening a small hole so I could see. I rolled down the window and drove slowly out of the parking lot. The wind was cold and damp as it came through the open window, and I debated closing it and taking a chance on running over something or someone in the fog. I finally decided to leave it open, at least until the windshield cleared.

A small decision but, as so often happens, a crucial one. Because I left the window open, in the next five minutes one life would end, one life would almost end, and one life would be saved.

As I came to a stop at the edge of the street, I heard a gunshot. Were I testifying in court, I would probably say I heard what I thought was a gunshot. If a cunning defense attorney asked me if I could have gotten the sound confused with a firecracker or the backfire of an automobile, I would have admitted the sounds are similar. But this was a gunshot. I was sure of it.

So sure I stopped the car and stepped out. I thought it came from the direction of the hospital, but it was hard to tell. As I stood in the clammy darkness, two figures emerged suddenly from the fog, running hard, one in front of the other, heading toward the vacant field across the street. As quickly as they appeared, they were gone, swallowed up by the misty darkness. I could hear the faint thud of running steps as they hit the street, then silence. They must be in the field.

My first thought was that I had witnessed some sort of altercation, a not-uncommon event at any county hospital with an emergency room. County hospitals tend to attract some of the rougher elements of our society, and our hospital was no exception.

I jumped back in the car and drove toward the area where the two men had headed. I turned into the field, and the car pitched and rolled over the rough ground, slamming me against the door as I went into a concealed gully. I slowed, trying to see past the fender-high weeds. I bounced across the seat, wishing I had fastened my seat belt, trying to dodge the larger holes, cursing the fog.

So far, I had seen nothing. My guess was that the two guys had run right through the field and were blocks away by now. The car dropped sickeningly, crashing into another gully. That did it. It was time to go. Then I saw them.

Two figures struggling on the ground. On top was a stocky, dark-headed man with thick arms, dressed in a green jump suit. He was fighting with a lanky man who was flat on his back underneath him. The man on the bottom was clearly getting the

178

worst of it. In the glare of the headlights, I could see blood streaking his face and a look of hopeless desperation in his eyes. He was also wearing a uniform.

I knew instantly what had occurred. The guy on top was a prisoner wearing a jailhouse jumpsuit. The one on the ground was a correction officer. No doubt he had been guarding the prisoner at the hospital when he broke and ran. The guard must have fired a warning shot, then decided he could outfight him. Obviously, he had not succeeded.

I threw the car into park and jumped out. I ran around behind the prisoner and looped my right arm around his neck. My plan was to pull him off the correction officer and then the two of us could subdue him. He looked pretty husky, but I thought we would be able to handle him.

Then I saw the gun.

The guard told me later he had tackled the fleeing prisoner, only to find himself quickly overmatched. He fought hard but, to his horror, felt the prisoner pull his gun from the holster. Fighting with all his strength, ignoring the pounding he was taking, he kept his hand locked on the cylinder, preventing the revolver from being fired. He told me he prayed that someone would come to his aid and was just seconds away from giving up when my car headlights appeared in the fog.

When I saw the gun, it was less than six inches away. The prisoner was trying to twist it around so he could shoot me in the face, but the guard hung on grimly, refusing to relinquish his grip.

Luckily, I am left-handed, so I was able to draw my own weapon. I put the barrel of my .38 under the man's nose and shouted, "Let go of the gun!"

He turned his head slightly, and I looked directly into his eyes. They were dark eyes: huge, round circles, empty and lifeless. "You'll have to kill me," he gasped, still struggling fiercely to get his gun free so he could shoot me.

All cops get used to the threats uttered by the people we deal

179

with. With experience, we soon learn who is serious and who is bluffing. This man was not bluffing. Every fiber of his being was dedicated to one thing: escape! I hesitated a second, hoping he would surrender. He fought harder, the gaping end of the gun an inch from my face.

I pushed the barrel of my revolver into his chest and pulled the trigger. The explosion as the gun fired was muffled by his clothing. He fell to one side, then struggled to his feet, clutching his chest. Blood suddenly fountained from his mouth, and I knew then the wound was a fatal one. He went to his knees, crawled forward, then collapsed. He shuddered and lay still.

The correction officer, his face bloody and bruised, stared at the body of the prisoner.

"Are you all right?" I asked.

He turned toward me, still dazed. "He tried to kill me," he said.

"I know. I'm glad I came along when I did." I keyed the radio. "109, headquarters. I've just shot a man. I'm across from University Hospital in the field. I need an ambulance out here, right away." There was an instant of breathless silence, then my transmission was acknowledged.

In seconds the field was swarming with deputies, paramedics, investigators, crime scene technicians, and the morbidly curious. Fred Kennedy, the identification technician, tapped me on the shoulder. "I'll need your gun for ballistics tests, Don." He extended a paper bag, and I placed the weapon in it carefully.

I went back to the office to give a recorded statement to Investigator Charles Joye. I must say I felt a little strange sitting in the interview room on the side of the desk where defendants usually sat. I had to wait a few minutes, and it was the first chance I had to take an inventory of my feeling. I decided my overwhelming emotion was relief. I had come so close to dying, I felt relieved that I was still alive. I was also glad I had done everything right.

The man I shot was awaiting trial on a variety of felony

charges. He had a detainer on him from Alabama and was a strong suspect in several recent armed robberies. He didn't have to die. He made a conscious choice not to surrender, even though his battle was over as soon as I drove up.

The rest of the investigation was completed quickly, and I was soon dismissed. Before I left, Lieutenant Steve Dunn, the officer in charge of the investigation, told me the state attorney would be holding an inquest the next afternoon to determine if the killing was justified. "Do you see any problems with it?" I asked.

He drew on his pipe. "Not a thing. I told the state attorney it was a clean shooting."

I drove home pondering the expression "clean shooting." It meant what it said. No complications. All the facts were easily verified. Only two witnesses. Clean. Easy to investigate. No controversy. A life ended. Cleanly. Only, it wasn't clean.

Death never is.

40

TRAFFIC STOP #4

The pretty blond looked up at me fearfully from the car.

"May I see your driver's license, please?"

Wordlessly, she took it from her billfold and handed it to me. I glanced at the name. "Miss Williams, I stopped you because you ran the red light back there and almost caused a serious accident."

Her beautiful eyes brimmed. "The light was yellow when I came to the intersection; I didn't mean to cause a problem." Tear drops rolled down her perfect cheeks.

I opened my ticket book, and she began to cry in earnest. "I'm sorry," she wailed piteously, "Can't you please give me another chance?" Her imploring face, bright with tears, was a sight to melt a heart of stone.

But my heart was not made of stone, and I had already made up my mind to write this lovely creature a ticket. For one thing, her explanation about the light being yellow was slightly at variance with the facts. Actually, the light was a blazing red and had been for a perceptible interval before her small white convertible rocketed through the intersection, accelerating to beat the traffic. Several drivers had to slam on their brakes to avoid hitting her. It was a miracle there had not been a wreck.

For another, I had been waiting for the light to change, too, and was one of those drivers forced to stand on the brakes. My brightly painted cruiser car should have stood out like a beacon, but either she had not seen it or had chosen to ignore it.

I made the turn and set off in pursuit. This was one ticket I was going to enjoy writing.

It required some effort, but after a mile or so, I pulled in behind her. The top was down on the car, and long blond hair streamed in the wind. I switched on the blue lights and yelped the siren a few times. She quickly pulled into the parking lot of a little beer joint.

As I stood by the car, writing the citation, several of the afternoon drinkers stepped out to observe the proceedings. The ravishing Miss Williams wept steadily, her wails of dismay clearly audible to the assembled crowd.

I could tell her performance was having an impact. There were mutters of disapproval from the group and the usual why-don't-they-put-some-criminals-in-jail-instead-of-picking-on-some-poor-girl kind of comments. When I thought the muttering was getting louder than necessary, I stopped writing and gave them a long look. They immediately ducked their heads and became totally absorbed in the composition of the parking lot. When a satisfactory level of silence had been achieved, I resumed writing.

I completed the citation and indicated where she was to sign. Sobbing as if her heart would break, she haltingly wrote her name and handed the book to me. "You have ten days to pay the fine or plead not guilty," I said.

Her tear-filled eyes opened wide with alarm. "My goodness, does this mean I'll have to go to court?"

"Not if you want to just pay the fine."

"But, good gracious, can't you give me a break, just this once?" Tears cascaded down her face.

"No, I can't. The citation is already written."

"Oh, please, please."

It was a powerful appeal, and for an instant I wavered, since I am somewhat susceptible to the entreaties of attractive women.

183

But the moment passed. I handed her license back and walked to my cruiser.

The little car's engine sputtered to life, and gears clashed as she shifted angrily. Her car began to move, then jerked to a stop.

She turned toward me, her beautiful face twisted in fury. "YOU BASTARD," she screamed, "I HOPE SOMEONE SHOOTS YOU!" With a spray of gravel the car sped away.

There was total silence among the group left in the parking lot. Finally, one of the men, a big-bellied tobacco chewer, loosed a brown stream and spoke for all of us when he said mildly, "Nice girl."

41

HOW TO CATCH AN ESCAPED PRISONER

"YOU'RE DEAD, PIG!" the frizzy-haired boy screeched. I looked into his wild, drug-crazed eyes, less than ten feet away. He was shirtless, revealing an emaciated torso wasted by chemical abuse. He was reaching for me, the needle tracks plainly visible on his thin arms. "You're dead," he shouted again.

I had to laugh, "So are you, lad, but you just don't know it."

He looked confused, then began to pound on the steel bars of the holding cell. "You're right, pig, I am dead." He giggled maniacally, "I'm dead, I'm dead..." he chanted, beating time on the bars.

I went back to writing my arrest report.

It was a busy afternoon. The jail was crowded with deputies booking prisoners; argumentative, belligerent arrestees demanding phone calls; harassed jailors running back and forth; and a swirling crowd of bondsmen and attorneys, all seeking a quick exit for their clients.

I was standing at the booking desk, finishing up the paperwork on a drunk I had just arrested, when a strained voice, trembling with urgency, came over the radio on my gunbelt. There was instant silence from all the deputies as we froze, waiting for the next transmission. When it came, the first few words were unintelligible, but I heard, "...and he's running south..." From

185

the out-of-breath sound of the voice, I guessed he was chasing someone on foot.

This was quickly confirmed. The shrill tones of the emergency alert signal were followed by the brisk voice of a female dispatcher, "Headquarters to all units: 78 had a prisoner get away from him at University Hospital, last seen heading south toward Leonard Street. Anyone in the area come in with your number."

There was a confused jabber of voices as nearby units tried to answer. I didn't bother with the radio; I just headed for the back door. The jail was only 100 yards from the hospital, and I was as close as anyone. Charlie Conners, a beefy patrol sergeant, was already jumping into his car as I sprinted around the corner. "Hop in with me," he shouted.

I threw myself into the front seat as he slammed the cruiser into reverse, smoking the tires. We squealed out of the driveway, turned on Leonard Street, and I spotted the prisoner immediately. Sprinting for the vacant field across from the hospital was a stocky, bearded man, a set of handcuffs dangling from one wrist. He had on a pullover sweatshirt with the sleeves cut out, and even at this distance, I could see the muscles bulging from his well-developed arms. He would be trouble in a fight.

The big Dodge engine strained as we careened across the road and into the field, the ear-splitting yelp of the siren making me wince. Seeing his escape cut off, the prisoner reversed direction. Conners jerked the wheel, and the heavy cruiser swung around, but we were in the field by then and doing about 50. We spun out in a cloud of dust, and the engine died. We both bailed out and took off after the guy. I heard other sirens in the distance, so there was no hope of permanent escape for our fleet-footed friend.

He wasn't going to give up easily, though. He headed back around the hospital again, then hesitated as two more cruisers slid to a stop in the parking lot. He turned toward us, and the loose handcuff flashed in the sun. I saw the desperation in his eyes and considered what kind of weapon the free handcuff would make, slashing into our faces. It wasn't a comforting thought.

There had been recent construction at this end of the hospital, and the ground was littered with pieces of scrap lumber. He bent down and came up clutching a four-foot plank. With a purposeful expression, he advanced towards us.

As far as I was concerned, this had gone quite far enough, thank you. Not only was this guy an escaped felon, he had, no doubt, assaulted one cop in making that escape and was now threatening us with his club.

We had all the justification we needed to turn the lad into a colander, and no one would have raised an eyebrow. Doubtless, Conners was thinking the same thing, because he reached for his gun as I went for mine. It was at that precise moment I made an interesting discovery.

I had no gun.

There was only an empty, gaping holster where there should have been the reassuring bulk of my .38.

I was fascinated how my brain processed this information. In the few milliseconds that had passed since I realized my gun was not there, I had rerun the previous events of the afternoon like a video recorder on fast rewind. Another millisecond and the tape recorder jarred to a stop, playing back the image of me locking my revolver in the outside security locker when I brought my drunk in. Since firearms are forbidden inside the jail, the lockers are provided for safe storage while we book our prisoners. I was sure mine was still there, safely nestled inside that locker, several hundred yards away.

A faint hope glimmered to life, then died abruptly when I glanced at Conners and saw him clutching the air in his holster, too. In our rush to get out the back door of the jail, we didn't think to stop at the lockers. Now neither one of us had a gun, and this person with the big club was about to seriously rearrange what little hair I had left.

I decided to run for the cruiser car and lock myself inside. It might be undignified, but it beat the hell out of having my brains splattered on my shoes. I took a step in that direction, when Conners bellowed, "Hold it right there, punk!" I froze, thinking for a moment he meant me.

The bearded batsman stopped too, his weapon upraised, looking at Conners, who still had his hand on the useless holster. "It's all over, son," Conners said, "Don't make me shoot you."

I almost burst out laughing. Shoot him? With what, for God's sake, his finger? But Conners didn't move a muscle. He just glared at the kid and kept his hand on his hip.

The prisoner looked around frantically, as if he wanted to make another run for it, but now several other deputies were running towards us. "Throw it down son," Conners said firmly, "we won't hurt you."

The guy stared at Conners for a few seconds, then his gaze wavered, and he let the board drop from his fingers. The other deputies took him into custody without difficulty.

With a loud *whoosh,* I let out the breath I discovered I had been holding for what seemed like an hour. "Great job, sarge," I said unsteadily.

Conners slapped me on the back and laughed, "Aw, hell, nothing to it."

I followed him back to the cruiser with some difficulty, because I found to my surprise my knees had turned to jelly donuts and would barely support my weight.

42

RAPE VICTIM

I was to meet a Mr. Alonzo Adams at a phone booth next to a Shell station. "109, it's supposed to be a rape, but we're having difficulty understanding the complainant," the dispatcher said.

A few minutes later, I turned into the Shell station. A whip-thin, grizzled man of indeterminate age was on one of the phones. He wore tattered, grease-stained work clothes and a faded Atlanta Braves baseball cap. I pulled up beside him and got out. His back was to me, and I tapped him on the shoulder. He turned slowly, trying to focus his bloodshot eyes, swaying back and forth. "Hold on a minute," he said into the receiver, "the sheriff is here." He placed the phone carefully on the shelf.

"Did you call the sheriff's department?" I asked.

"Yeah, they on the phone." He reached for the receiver and knocked it off. It swung on the end of the cord while he tried unsuccessfully to grab it.

I reached past him and picked it up. "This is Parker."

"Thank God!" the dispatcher said, "I haven't been able to understand a word he was saying. Good luck."

I hung up and turned back to the guy. "What's the problem, Mr. Adams?"

He was still staring at the phone. I snapped my fingers in front of him. "Hey, over here." He turned. "What's the trouble?"

He belched. "It's a rape."

"Who got raped?"

He thought about this for a moment, frowning as he concentrated. Finally he said, "My woman."

"Your wife?"

He shook his head, "No, my woman."

"Where is she?"

He made a vague gesture. "Back at the trailer."

It was only a few blocks away, and as we drove he said his woman told him she had been raped and demanded he call the cops. He had to walk to the pay phone, so it took some time for him to make the report. He was exceptionally intoxicated, and I had a difficult time understanding him.

We pulled up in front of a crumbling mobile home which was jammed into a tiny, trash-filled lot behind a closed paint-and-body shop. The rusted remains of several dozen cars blended well with the faded blue trailer and the scattered tire carcasses.

We stepped into the small living room. Stacks of newspapers, dirty clothes, moldy dishes, and a layer of empty beer cans littered the floor. The couch was an old car seat, propped up on concrete blocks, several springs spurting from the torn upholstery. The place smelled like an ash tray in a beer joint. Adams stepped through the rubble, the floor creaking beneath him. "Hey, Gertie, the sheriff is here."

I followed him into the bedroom at the end of the trailer. In the dim light, I could see a still form on the bed. The form was snoring loudly. Adams sat down heavily on the bed. "Gertie, wake up."

The body began to come to life, snorting and coughing. A mass of mouse-brown hair rose from the mottled sheets. It was a female of the same species as Adams. "Where the hell you been?" she croaked.

"The law's here." he said.

Gertie stared at me for a long time. Finally, she pushed Adams, "Get out of the way." Obediently, he slid to the foot of the bed.

She worked her bony legs out from under the covers and stood up. At first I thought she was wearing socks, but then realized her feet were so filthy it only looked like socks. She had on a ragged slip and nothing else. Every rib was visible, and her hip bones looked sharp enough to slice meat.

"Ma'am, Mr. Adams says you've been raped."

Her eyes widened. "Raped?"

"That's what he told me."

She looked at Adams, who nodded gravely. This seemed to jog her memory. "Yes, sir," she said enthusiastically, "I sure have been raped."

"Who raped you?"

She whirled and pointed dramatically at Adams. "He did!"

This was getting good. "When did he rape you?"

She thought a moment. "It happened today."

I turned to Adams. "Is that right?" He nodded agreeably. "Why did you rape her?"

He considered my question. "She wanted me to."

"I did not!" she cried. "I told him to get us some beer. I didn't want to do no moochin'."

I smiled, "What's 'mooching'?"

She sighed, "Thass all he think about. He's like every man I ever knowed."

"How long have you two been living together?"

She turned to him. "Lonzo, how long we been together?"

"I reckon it been 'bout five years."

"Has he ever raped you before, ma'am?"

She nodded vigorously. "Yes, sir. He raped me plenty of times before, ain't you, 'Lonzo?"

Adams smiled. "Sure."

"Do you think he'll rape you again?"

"Yes, SIR!" She said emphatically. "Soon as you leave."

"Are you going to rape Gertie when I leave, Mr. Adams?"

He nodded. "Well, I 'spect so, but I ain't as young as I used to be. Time was I could rape her two, three times a day."

191

I laughed. "Oh, I'm sure you're just being modest."

"No, he ain't modern." Gertie said. "He just rape me the same way he always done."

"I guess it's caused you a lot of problems, then?"

"Yes, sir. He just rapes me and rapes me. I can't get no relief."

"Well, I'm afraid we're going to have to begin an intensive investigation. It could take months."

She sighed dolefully, "Thass what I was afraid of. So now I got to stay here with 'Lonzo while he rapes me some more." Adams smiled happily.

"Yes, I guess you will."

She crawled back into the bed. "Well, you done the best you could. I sure 'preciate you coming."

"My pleasure, ma'am."

"You gonna tell me when the 'vestigation is done?"

"We'll notify you."

"Thass good, 'cause 'Lonzo prob'ly gonna rape me again soon as you leave."

"I sure hope not."

She sighed again. "Thass all right. I'm used to it."

43

WHAT HAPPENED
LAST NIGHT

Because I am a cop, people naturally expect me to know all the details about every law enforcement happening.

Throughout the entire county.

24 hours a day.

It never seems to occur to them that I do not work 24 hours a day. It also does not seem to occur to them that I work only for the sheriff's department and not every agency in the area.

I am constantly being quizzed about incidents of which I have only the vaguest notion. If it wasn't for TV, radio, and the newspapers, I probably wouldn't be as well-informed as I am.

After years of being grilled about things I knew nothing about, I devised a new strategy to better deal with the problem. It was intended to prevent those long, unproductive conversations I kept having with curious people.

The conversations generally started out the same way. "Say, Don," someone would ask, an eager, expectant look on his face, "where were all those cop cars going last night?"

Now if I am going to answer this question, I'm going to have to obtain just a bit more information. "What time was it when you saw the cars?"

"Um . . . it must have been about 8:00. . . or it might have been 5:30. Actually, I think it was closer to 10." He'd wait.

"I don't remember anything big happening last night."

"Oh, this was big, all right. There must have been five or six cars, going like hell, blue lights, sirens, the whole bit. Of course, if it's something you can't talk about. . ."

"No, no. It's nothing like that. I just can't recall anything around that time." I'd try again. "Were they sheriff's department cars or police department cars?"

"They might have been, or they could have been state troopers." He'd smile, pleased he had cleared up the confusion.

Eventually, there came a time when I had to shut off this torrent of non-information by confessing I had no idea where all the cop cars were going in such a hurry last night. The reaction was invariably the same: he'd leave, convinced I was refusing to tell him.

After several years of this, I gave up. They wanted answers, they got answers. When I was asked, "Where were all those cars going last night?" I would say tersely, "Double axe murder."

"Double axe murder?"

"Yeah, brains, blood, and eyeballs, all over the place."

"My God! What happened?"

At this point, I usually tried to personalize the story. As the narrator, I felt it my duty to impart a moral lesson for the benefit of my listener. If I knew of some personal weakness on his part, I tried to work it into the story line in such a way it fit my inquisitive friend to a "T," but seemed a mere coincidence.

"The guy's wife did it."

"His wife? I can't believe it."

"Yeah, it was kind of funny. She warned him about watching too much football on TV. They were supposed to go out and celebrate their anniversary, but he wouldn't leave the game. He and one of his buddies just sat there, sucking up the suds." I'd give him a thin smile. "I guess something snapped, because she chopped up both of them. Poor guys didn't have a chance."

While he was digesting this little tidbit, I would say

194

conversationally, "By the way, how are you and Marge getting along?"

The look on his face usually made further comment unnecessary.

If I knew a bit more about my friend's personal life than he realized, I might try a different approach. When he asked about the identity of the axe swinger, I might say,

"His girlfriend did it."

"His girlfriend?"

"Yeah. Seems as though he had been promising for months to divorce his wife and marry her. I guess she finally got tired of it. She killed him and his wife. Can you imagine a woman doing something like that?"

If I was on target, my man usually gulped, agreeing he couldn't imagine such a thing.

While I cheerfully admit these tales were fabricated, I must say I had more satisfied customers than when I told the truth. I did have a few people ask me why it hadn't been in the paper, but I could usually head this one off by saying scornfully, "Hell, you know how the news media is!"

They would nod, not wanting to be thought of as some sort of bleeding-heart liberal.

I used my double-axe-murder story so often I began to forget who I told it to. Once I had a guy say, "Good Lord, isn't that the third double axe murder this year?"

After that, I added a few new tales of horror to prevent duplication.

So, don't ever ask me where all those cruiser cars were going last night . . . unless you want an answer.

44

THE NIGHT OF
THE CHAIR LEG

It had been a brutal 3:00 to 11:00 P.M. shift, and I could barely keep up with the calls. I finished up a family fight and reported myself back in service.

"109?"

I sighed. "Go ahead."

"Contact the head nurse on the fourth floor of the Specialty Care Center. They have a male psychiatric patient who has gone berserk and is tearing the place apart. One of the nurses has been injured."

Wonderful! No doubt, no one else would be available to back me up. I acknowledged the call.

"Back to 109."

"Go ahead."

"10-4, 109, all the other units are tied up right now, so we don't have anyone free for a backup."

"That's 10-4, thank you very much."

Taking care of major disturbances at psychiatric wards is just one of the fun things deputies get to do, but we don't get called for the minor stuff. The situation must be truly serious.

If you are thinking the cops are called to the bad situations because we are walking arsenals, please disabuse yourself of this thought immediately. We are not allowed to carry weapons onto psychiatric wards. No guns, no blackjacks, no flashlights, no nothing, because there is always the chance a violent patient could take the weapon away from us.

Just to help us sleep better at night, we all know that, if a certifiable psychotic stomps us into a grease spot, he will never be prosecuted. Remember why he is in the hospital to start with. He's a nut, right? If he's nutty enough, he might not be held legally responsible for his actions.

All this was in my mind as I headed toward the hospital. I was only a few blocks away and arrived within moments. I left my gun at the admissions office, and I must say, I was not thrilled with the welcome I got from the nervous receptionist. "Are you the only one?" she asked.

"I'm it," I said. "Everyone else is busy."

"But we asked for at least four deputies; this man is extremely violent." My stomach lurched, but I tried not to look as alarmed as I felt.

I got off the elevator on the fourth floor, expecting to find chaos. Instead I found it quiet. Eerily so. A nurse met me as I stepped out. "Thank God you've come." She looked past me, "Where are the others?"

I was getting a little tired of this question. "I'm afraid I'm the only one available. Everyone else is busy." She shook her head, and my nervousness increased by leaps and bounds. I knew this nurse. She was a real pro, not one to cry wolf. If SHE was upset, then so was I. "What's the situation?"

"A patient attacked the medications nurse, but she managed to get away. He was down at the end of the hall smashing up the furniture, but he's been quiet for the last few minutes."

The elevator opened behind me, and I jumped. A thin black man about 50, dressed in a white uniform stepped out. The nurse said, "I asked Mr. Smith to come up. He's the orderly tonight."

Mr. Smith smiled, "How ya doing?"

"I've been better," I said sourly.

He smiled again, "I'm sure we can handle him." I was not

197

at all convinced of this. Mr. Smith looked as though a strong wind would blow him away.

"You know karate or anything?" I asked hopefully.

He laughed, "Naw, man, I don't know no karate, but I ain't going to let no nut hurt me, neither."

I walked to the doors leading into the ward and peered through the window. The hall was deserted, but there was an "L" at the end of the hall. I suspected our man was out of sight around that corner. Nothing to do but go in and find out if he was really as violent as he was said to be.

The nurse unlocked the heavy doors to the ward. Smith and I stepped through, and she quickly locked them behind us. We started down the long hall. I felt like a western marshal heading for a shoot-out. It was not a pleasant feeling.

There was no sound except for our footsteps and the hammering of my heart. We were about halfway down the hall when Smith said, "Uh-oh." I had been busy looking into the other rooms as we passed, because I didn't want the patient to ambush us from behind. When Smith spoke, I whipped around so fast I almost broke my neck. A stocky guy in a hospital gown was peering at us from around the wall at the end of the corridor. He didn't look too big. I figured we could take him.

Then he stepped out into the hall. He was holding a chunk of lumber at least three feet long. It was slightly curved, and a large bolt protruded from the end. It was a chair leg.

We came to a stop. I don't know why Smith stopped, but I stopped because I was totally paralyzed with terror. The guy shuffled toward us, his eyes burning holes through me. We took a few steps back. I was all for running for the door and screaming hysterically, but before I could do so, Smith suddenly darted into a room to his right. Great, I thought: He's going to leave me here to be killed first.

I was about to make a break for it when Smith emerged from the room. He was holding a chair in front of him like a shield and advancing on the club-swinger. "Get around behind him," he said quietly. I got the idea. If the guy came after me, Smith would cream him with the chair. If he went after Smith, I could jump him.

The nut realized this, too, because he took a few steps back, trying to watch both of us. I kept circling, and the guy kept backing up. Finally, we had him in a corner. He looked at Smith and he looked at me, then simply threw the club down. In short order, we had him back in his room and tightly restrained. The guy never said a word.

Back outside I thanked Smith profusely for saving my life, but he just smiled, "Nothing to it, my man. I figured we could handle him."

45

AS THE TWIG IS BENT

"Want some coffee, Don?"

I turned, not believing my ears. Was Sergeant Swinney actually offering to get me some coffee? It was only fair, since I had just finished booking the drunk he had arrested, but it was still hard to believe. "Yeah, I'd really like some coffee, Sarge."

"Me, too," he said with a broad smile. "Make mine black."

A nearby correction officer exploded with laughter, "Boy, he really got you that time, didn't he, Parker?"

"He gets me every time," I grumbled as I went to fetch the coffee. Some day I would be the sergeant, and I would have hardworking, dedicated subordinates like me to order around. When that day arrived, I would run them ragged getting me coffee.

I was heading back to the booking counter, balancing the hot cups gingerly, when a group of prisoners shuffled by, hands shackled to waist chains, ankles hobbled by leg restraints. I stepped back to let them pass. The correction officer leading the procession opened the door to the holding cell. Bound for the state prison, they would wait here for the prison bus to arrive.

I gave Swinney his coffee. "Thank you, Deputy Parker," he said with exaggerated politeness. I grimaced and turned away as he chuckled. I stood at the counter sipping my coffee. Someone in the holding cage laughed, and I glanced at the prisoners, then

200

looked again. There was something vaguely familiar about one of them.

The man who had drawn my attention was a tall, gaunt, redhead about twenty-five-years old. The homemade tattoos on his arms and the sullen, wary expression on his face told me he had been down this road before. I stared at him for a few moments, trying to recall where I had seen that face.

Then I remembered.

It was in the fall of 1970, and I was a rookie deputy sheriff assigned to the radio room as a communications dispatcher. Since I was so new, I spent most of my time taking reports from people who came to the sheriff's department with various problems.

This particular day had been a busy one, and I had spent most of the last hour with the phone jammed in my ear. The woman entered the lobby timidly and stood quietly, waiting for me to finish. Middle-aged and plump, she reminded me of my third grade Sunday school teacher. When I finally hung up, she stepped forward uncertainly and placed a framed picture on the counter. I glanced at it, and a handsome red-haired teenager stared back at me, his clear-blue eyes a carbon copy of his mother's.

"What's the problem, ma'am?"

"It's my son," she said, twisting her fingers. "He's run away."

It was a familiar story. The rebellious teenager, skipping school, running with a bad crowd, minor scrapes with the law, and now he had run away. "But he's really a good boy," she assured me, wiping a tear from her cheek. I took the necessary information, slid the photograph out of the frame and paper-clipped it to the report.

The kid was found within a few days, and the picture returned to his mother.

Two months later I saw the picture attached to another runaway report, but this time it stayed in the file for months. Every day I came to work and looked through the reports, and every day I saw those blue eyes looking back at me.

Eventually, I was transferred out of the radio room and took my place in the patrol division. Interestingly enough, I still heard the kid's name from time to time, because he was staying in trouble. Every so often, he would be arrested for one thing or another, and each offense was more serious than the last.

Eventually, he turned 18, which meant he was now treated as an adult. Heavily into drugs, he was finally sent to state prison. Back on the streets, he was arrested again less than a month after being released, and the last I heard, he was back in prison. But that had been ten years ago.

I walked to the holding cage and called his name. He looked up. I saw his eyes were still bright blue, but they had a disturbing flatness to them now. He stared at me without curiosity. To him, I was just another cop.

I told him I had taken that first runaway report back in 1970. He laughed and shook his head. "Yeah, I remember. My mother was really freaking out over that one."

"What are you going back to prison for?"

"Armed robbery," he said matter-of-factly, "I was strung out, and I don't even remember it." As he moved his arms I saw the scars and dimples of the needle tracks.

"How much time did you get?" I asked.

He looked at me steadily, then said, "Life."

The prison bus pulled up outside, and the group moved slowly out of the cell to be searched before boarding. I stood beside him for a moment, trying to think of something more to say. Finally, I said, "Your mother always said you were a good boy."

He smiled slightly, "Yeah, well, she was wrong."

The heavy security door rumbled open, and the men shuffled toward the waiting bus. "Good luck," I said. He didn't reply.

46

THE DAY OF THE LIZARD

"Hey, Don!" Mike bellowed.

I turned to the stocky cook, "What?"

"Telephone."

I left my breakfast reluctantly. It was bound to be the dispatcher. Who else would be calling at six o'clock on a chilly winter morning? Who else even knew I was here? I could only hope it would be a low-priority call, one which would allow me to finish those glorious blueberry hotcakes, dripping with melted butter and swimming in maple syrup. The two quick bites I had taken were not nearly enough.

I picked up the receiver. "Parker."

No one answered, but I could hear laughter in the background. Lots of laughter. People were yelling back and forth, but I couldn't make out the words. Something was sure funny, though; it sounded like a party. "HELLO?" I shouted.

That got a response. "Oh, Don," a dispatcher said, gasping for breath, "have we got a call for you!"

"Great," I said sourly, "I can hardly wait."

"But you're going to love it, and it's an emergency."

"There must be three or four fatalities, judging from the amount of hilarity."

He repeated my bit of sarcasm, and the rest of the dispatchers burst into fresh shrieks of laughter. My irritation grew as I waited for this baying hyena to give me the call.

Finally regaining control he said, "A woman at lot 41, Shady Grove Trailer Park, called. She said there was an animal in her trailer, and she needs help."

"What kind of animal?"

He started chuckling again, "We think it's a lizard."

"A what?"

He was laughing, "A lizard: you know, about six inches long. They eat bugs."

I was not amused. "I know what a lizard is, but why does she need a deputy?"

"Well, she's about half-hysterical. We don't know if she's looney or what, but she damn sure wants a deputy and fast."

"What the hell am I supposed to do with a lizard?"

"You can always shoot it."

"Very funny."

He was still chuckling, "You've got the call."

"Thanks a lot."

"Oh, don't mention it, and Don?"

"What?"

"Be careful." Laughter reverberated as I hung up.

A lizard. In a trailer. What fun. I gazed longingly at my beautiful hotcakes, sitting in lonely splendor on the table, now destined for the garbage can. They deserved a better fate.

I pulled out of the parking lot and headed east, into the sun that was inching above the horizon. A few moments later I turned into the trailer park and started looking for number 41. The last trailer on the row was a large double-wide which hadn't been there long. The ground was still raw around the plumbing connections, and there were deep ruts made by the tires. At the same instant I spotted the number, I saw a sight that will be forever etched in my memory.

The door was standing open, and there beside the trailer, illuminated by the cool light of dawn, was a very attractive lady wearing frilly shorty pajamas, her long, slender legs accentuated by lacy panties. She stood barefoot on the frosty grass, her hair in bulky rollers, covered with something that looked like a shower cap.

I was so thunderstruck by this vision I almost drove through the fence. She began waving frantically, and I managed to get my car stopped without wrecking it. I stepped out, and she ran across the yard, long legs flashing in the sun, her curlers bobbing and clattering.

Any other woman would have been dying from embarrassment, but not this one. She had an expression of such utter horror I knew she was not the least bit concerned that she was essentially half-naked in front of a stranger. There were more pressing things on her mind.

She grabbed me by the arm. "Oh, my God, I thought you'd never get here. What took you so long? I called 15 minutes ago. You've got to help me!" The words tumbled out in a confused babble.

"What's the trouble, ma'am?" I said, trying to look at her face.

She stared at me incredulously. "What's the trouble? I told that man on the phone what the trouble was." She pointed at the trailer and said fearfully, "There's an animal in there."

I studied the open door warily. Her near-panic was beginning to affect me. A grown woman wouldn't be carrying on like this because of a lizard. No, there must be something else. The dispatchers must have made a mistake.

"What kind of animal?" I asked nervously.

"I'm not sure, but I think it's an alligator."

"An alligator?"

She flushed, no small accomplishment, considering the temperature. "Well, it's a small alligator."

"Where is it?"

She took a deep breath. "It's in the dining room, by the table."

I nodded. Nothing to do now but see for myself. I walked toward the trailer, watching the doorway intently. I did not for one minute believe there was actually an alligator in her dining room, but I was still nervous. The lady had been badly frightened by something.

I peered inside the door, hand on my revolver, but I saw nothing. She followed as I stepped carefully inside. I was standing in the living room of the attractively furnished mobile home. The kitchen-dining area was to my left, and I scanned every inch of it looking for anything slithering or crawling. Nothing.

I breathed a little easier. Maybe this was just another nut call. I was about to make a light-hearted remark about disappearing alligators, when the woman let out a blood-curdling scream and leaped out the open door. I was right behind her.

"My God, what is it?" I said, trying to get my breathing under control.

"It was there, on the back of the chair," she wailed, "I saw it move."

I had seen nothing. "What the hell was it?"

She drew a shuddering breath. "Like I said, I think it's an alligator."

I repeated my cautious entry to the trailer, but this time I unsnapped my holster. I had seen no alligators, but her reaction had taken three years off my life, and I was taking no chances.

As I stood by the kitchen counter, searching the room with my eyes, my attention was drawn by the tiniest flash of movement on the back of one of the dining room chairs. At first I didn't see anything. The vinyl-covered chair had a green floral print, and the thing I was looking for blended in. It moved again and I saw it.

There, on the back of the chair, was a bright green lizard, perhaps five inches long from the tip of his scaly nose to the end of his slender tail. It was a common chameleon or anole, capable of turning brown or green depending on the background it was occupying. Right now, it was well camouflaged on the green chair. What this little fellow was doing in this lady's trailer on this cold morning was a question without an answer.

THE DAY OF THE LIZARD

"Ma'am, I've found the animal."

"Can you shoot it?" she asked from outside the trailer.

I laughed. "I don't think that will be necessary; I'll just catch it for you."

"I don't want it!"

"I meant, I'll get it out of the trailer." I crept up to the chair and snatched the lizard off the back, cupping it in my hands. The woman worked up enough courage to step back inside. She stood in the doorway, shivering from the cold and from fear, watching me with wide eyes.

"It's okay, I've caught him." I held up my hands, and she shrank back in horror. Playfully, I made a quick motion, as though to toss the lizard at her. With an ear-splitting shriek, she catapulted out the door and into the yard. It was an amazing display of athletic agility, made even more impressive by her scanty costume.

I stepped outside, and she scuttled around my car. I was feeling bad because she was so obviously terrified. "Don't worry, I'm not going to throw it at you."

She wasn't convinced and kept the car between us. I found a used styrofoam coffee cup in my car and put the lizard in it, snapping the lid on tightly. "See," I said, displaying the cup, "no more lizard."

She relaxed slightly. "What are you going to do with it?"

"I'll let it go in some bushes."

Her eyes rolled in alarm, "Not around here?"

"No, no. I'll take him far away, I promise."

"Thank God." She drew a long breath. "My husband and I just moved down here from Maine. He's at work, and I didn't know who else to call."

I stared at her. "Don't they have bears and wolves and things like that in Maine?"

"Oh, sure," she said, "but they don't have alligators that get in your house."

"It's not an alligator," I laughed. "It's just a lizard. They're all over the place down here.''

"Oh, my God,'' she whispered.

"But they won't hurt you,'' I said hastily. "Actually, they are quite beneficial. They eat bugs.''

She thanked me for removing the lizard, and I watched appreciatively as she walked back inside, then I drove off. As soon as I was out of sight, I released the lizard and headed for the office, shaking my head at the lovely lady in the shorty pajamas, terrorized by a lizard.

47

THE HORSE IN
THE SUNSET MOTEL

The second fire engine went by, siren wailing, festooned with clinging firemen. "Headquarters," I said into the microphone, "are you SURE you don't have a report of a fire?"

"Negative, 109, we have no report of . . . standby." I didn't standby, I was already following the trucks up the highway.

"109?"

"Go ahead, I'm right behind the fire trucks."

"10-4, we do have a report of a fire."

I chuckled, "I'll bet it's at the Sunset Motel, right?" This was not exactly a lucky guess on my part, since I could see the glow of the flames from my car.

"That's 10-4," she said, unruffled by my sarcastic tone. "The call is assigned to you."

I acknowledged and turned into the driveway of the Sunset. One of the cottages was on fire. Seriously on fire. Roaring flames were completely engulfing the small structure. The only thing the fire department could do here was try and save the adjacent cottages.

I was grateful for the heat from the blaze as I stepped from my warm car into the twenty-degree January night. I walked toward the burning building and had the strange sensation of freezing on one side and roasting on the other. I found I could face toward the fire, then away, and stay partially comfortable.

I was on my second rotation when I saw the apparition.

Off to one side of the flaming cottage, wrapped only in a bed sheet, was a shivering, emaciated man, who looked as though he had just crawled out of a box car after a transcontinental journey. He was swaying back and forth, and I went over to see if he was injured. "Hey, are you all right?"

He turned toward me, clutching the sheet, staring with vacant eyes. Up close, I saw he was filthy. He probably hadn't had a shave in two weeks or a bath in three. It was also obvious he had been on intimate terms with a substantial quantity of strong drink in the not-too-distant past.

"Are you all right?" I repeated.

His eyes focused on my uniform, and he grabbed my arm. "You've got to get him out!" he said desperately.

My God! Someone was still in there. I looked at the smoking cottage as the last wall collapsed in a shower of sparks. There was no chance. "I'm sorry, there's nothing we can do now," I said in a low voice.

His eyes filled with tears, "Can't you help him?"

"Who was he?"

"My horse," he sobbed.

That gave me a jolt. "Your horse?"

"Yeah, I brought him inside because of the cold." Overcome with grief, he had to stop a moment as his shoulders heaved with sobs. Regaining some of his composure, he said, "I woke up and there was fire; fire was everywhere!"

My head reeled, a horse? In the Sunset Motel? Well, stranger things had happened. I told the weeping man to sit in the front seat of my cruiser, before he froze to death.

I was a little unsure of what to do next. I didn't really have the guts to tell one of the firemen I thought there might be a dead horse in the smoldering ashes of the cottage. I could well imagine their reaction, particularly if no horse was found. I decided to find the motel manager. He ought to know if there really was a horse.

I found him standing by a fire truck, cupping a mug of coffee like a hand warmer. I gave him a friendly smile. He didn't return it. "Hi, how ya doing?" I said.

"I'm freezing my ass off, how are you doing?" He took a noisy slurp of coffee.

"Yeah, me, too," I said, blowing on my hands. "Uh, listen. That guy sitting in my cruiser car over there says he had a horse in the room with him."

The manager took another sip of coffee and said calmly, "I'm sure he did."

I was thunderstruck. "You mean he really did have a horse in his room?"

He gave a sharp laugh. "Yeah, and an elephant, a gorilla, and a dozen snakes, all pink."

"Wha...what do you mean?"

"He's seeing things." He laughed again. "He's just one of our regular drunks holed up for the weekend." He gestured toward the now-leveled cottage. "Do you know what the silly bastard did?"

I shook my head.

"He made a fire in the heater. Crumpled up some newspapers, broke up one of the chairs and threw it in, then touched a match to it and went to bed."

"So?"

"It's a gas space heater, not a fireplace. By rights, he should have burned to death." He shook his head. "You didn't believe that crap about the horse, did you?"

I flushed. "Oh, hell, no," I said hastily. "I figured the guy was wacko right from the start."

"You gonna put him in jail?"

I looked at the trembling wreck, still crying his eyes out, in the front seat of my cruiser. "Yeah, I guess so. I can probably figure out some sort of negligent arson charge."

He snorted, "It don't make any difference to me. I don't own this dump. They want me to rent to winos, they ought to expect to burn a few rooms down.''

"Well, in that case, I'll just charge him with public drunk (a crime, in those less-enlightened days). At least he'll have some place warm to sleep." I turned to go.

"Hey!"

I looked back. He chuckled, "Wouldn't it be great if we really DID find a dead horse in there?''

I was not amused. "If that happens, you call me."

I backed out of the driveway with the drunk sobbing beside me and the manager still standing beside the fire truck, laughing at the thought of a horse in the Sunset Motel.

48

HIGH-SPEED CHASE

Few things will get a cop's adrenalin flowing quicker than a high-speed chase. This is one thing television and movies portray accurately. No matter how fanciful a chase scene seems to be, I am convinced that some cop has experienced a real-life chase that matches or exceeds it.

I was still in training, riding as a passenger with a veteran, the first time I experienced the gut-wrenching excitement of a true high-speed chase. Another deputy had tried to stop a car for a routine traffic violation, but the driver took off. I never forgot the tremendous surge of excitement when I heard his high-pitched yell, "He's running from me!" echo from the radio speaker. It was a battle cry I would hear many more times in my career, and one I would utter myself occasionally.

In this case, we were only a few blocks away and quickly joined the pursuit. We rocketed around the curves, barely staying on the road, while the pursuing deputy kept up a steady commentary on his position so everyone would know where he was. One of the big dangers was the real possibility of collision with another cruiser car speeding to his assistance. We caught occasional glimpses of his blue lights when we would hit a straight, and it looked as we were gaining on him.

As we approached a particularly treacherous series of curves, his commentary ended abruptly. Tires squalling, we slid through the turns. As we straightened, I was astounded to see the pursuing deputy's cruiser car upside down at the side of the road, front tires still spinning slowly, steam rising in clouds from the ruptured radiator.

Luckily, the deputy was not seriously injured, although his car was totalled. The guy we were chasing made it another mile or so before he wrecked, too, and that points out an essential truth about high-speed chases: if the pursuit lasts long enough, someone is going to bend a car. Sometimes it's the good guys, sometimes the bad guys, sometimes both.

The reason for the chase is frequently a mystery. It could be the fleeing driver is an escaped convict, a recent bank robber, or a car thief. It could be he is a smart-alec teenager who has been watching too much television and wants to show off for his girlfriend. If the only charges that can be confirmed are a slew of traffic violations, frequently the best course of action is to break off the pursuit in the interests of safety.

But that's hard to do. It's almost a slap in our macho faces to let safety be the better part of valor. We watch television, too, and we know Clint Eastwood, John Wayne, or Steve McQueen would never give up the pursuit just because a few dozen taxpayers might be eliminated.

One particular chase which occurred a good many years ago taught me about the unpredictability of drivers. It took place during the early morning hours of an otherwise uneventful midnight shift.

I was sitting at a red light when I first saw the battered old Chevrolet moving slowly through the parking lot of the shopping center. Lights off, the car came around the corner of the building, headed toward the road. Very suspicious. I cut across the parking lot to intercept the car. I flipped on my blue lights and lit up the the interior of the vehicle with my spotlight. The driver turned toward me, eyes wide with apprehension.

Before I could tell the radio room I was about to check out

a suspicious car, the vehicle lunged forward, sparks flying from the muffler as he bounced over the curb. Cursing, I spun the wheel of my cruiser, trying to get turned around. He had caught me by surprise.

By the time I got straightened out, he was two blocks ahead, belching clouds of oily smoke as he roared away. "109 to headquarters!" I shouted into the microphone, "I've got a vehicle running from me." I gave the direction of travel, and the dispatcher instantly put the station on emergency traffic to give me a clear frequency.

The old car wasn't able to go very fast, and I quickly closed the distance. He made a sliding turn, and the car heeled drunkenly. I thought he was going to roll over, but he managed to stay upright and, tires spinning, straightened out and headed down the road. I took the corner smoothly, the heavy-duty suspension of my cruiser letting me get around quickly, and now I was right behind him.

This whole time I was trying to figure out why he was running from me. My guess was that he had broken into one of the businesses in the shopping center. But, no matter my suspicions, all I had him for at this point was a rapidly accumulating list of traffic violations. We shot through a red light at seventy, and I mentally added the light to the list.

A few blocks down the road, he wheeled into a left turn, but, at 50 miles an hour, the big Chevy didn't wheel too well. The car started to slide, and I saw his frantic movements as he spun the steering wheel, desperately trying to regain control, but it was hopeless.

The car slid through the intersection and crashed into a small tree. There was an explosion of glass, wood splinters, and leaves, as the tree trunk sheared off and the car went over, coming to rest on the driver's side.

I leaped from my cruiser, gun drawn, and approached the crumpled Chevy.

"Don't shoot!" a shaky voice called out. I looked through

the hole where the windshield had been and saw a figure trying to untangle himself from the ruined car.

"Come on out of there," I said. "And keep your hands in sight."

He crawled through the gap left by the windshield. He was a young guy, bruised and battered but otherwise unhurt. He stood up slowly, both hands high in the air, looking very scared.

I patted him down for weapons, got him handcuffed, and read him his rights. He readily agreed to talk but steadfastly denied he was a burglar. "Then why did you run from me?" I asked him.

He lowered his head and said softly, "I ain't got no driver's license."

I could only shake my head in wonder as I placed him in the back of my cruiser car. He had come within a whisker of being killed, simply because he didn't want to get a ticket. It was amazing.

49

TRAFFIC STOP #5

BEEEEEP - The horn blared angrily as the outraged driver stamped on his brakes to avoid the big Ford which had just run the red light.

Unfortunately, I was witness to the whole thing, since I was only two blocks from the intersection. I say "unfortunately", because now I would be forced to take action. Don't misunderstand my lack of enthusiasm. I'm willing to do my job, but it had been a long, hot day, and I was looking forward to getting off. I made up my mind that, unless this guy started shooting at me, I would let him off with a warning.

I flipped on the blue lights, eased through the intersection, and chased the guy down within a few blocks.

As I walked up to the car, I saw a teenaged girl in the front seat and a younger girl in the back. Both watched me approach with wide-eyed fascination while the man, whom I presumed to be their father, fumbled for his license.

Before I could say anything, he handed me the license and said loudly, "I'm glad you stopped me; yes, sir, I'm really glad you did, because it shows you are doing your job like you should."

I was completely taken aback. I have heard just about every reaction possible from people stopped for traffic violations, but never before had someone expressed pleasure. "I'm glad you're so happy about it," I said, mystified at his good humor.

"I certainly am," he said briskly. "A traffic violation is a serious matter."

I was beginning to believe I was dealing with a lunatic here. What else could explain his actions? I looked at him more closely. He didn't seem psychotic.

"I also think you acted very promptly," he continued. "After all, I might have caused a wreck back there."

"No doubt about it." I agreed. Definitely a loony.

He turned to the girls, "I hope this will be a good lesson for both of you. If you violate the law, you have to expect to pay the consequences." They both nodded solemnly.

"Well, I'm glad you're so understanding about this," I said. "Since you recognize how dangerous your driving was, I'm willing to let you go with a warning this time, but if..."

"Oh, no," he interrupted, "I insist you write me a ticket." He waved his hand toward the two girls, "It's as much for their benefit as anything else."

I bent down so I could see the older girl. I wanted to see if she was as buggy as her old man.

She looked back at me with luminous brown eyes. "Daddy was teaching me to drive," she said.

Instantly, it all became clear. His strange behavior, his loud, lecturer style of speaking, his forced good humor. Of course. The poor devil had probably chewed out his kid for some goof and then taken the wheel himself. Still fuming, he must have tried to beat the light to ease his frustration, with this disastrous result.

Crazed with guilt and mortified at being stopped, he must be clinging tenaciously to the twisted logic that somehow he could make amends by having me write him a citation.

I could only imagine the fate that awaited him when his gleeful daughters spread the news far and wide that daddy had gotten a ticket while teaching sis how to drive.

What could I do? From the slight edge of hysteria in his voice, I fully expected him to create a major scene if I didn't write him a ticket. At the least, he would probably complain to the sheriff. The thought of explaining why I refused to give a ticket to someone requesting one was too bizarre to contemplate.

I opened my citation book and began to write. Through it all, he kept up a steady stream of moralizing to the girls about the necessity of taking responsibility for one's own actions, the inevitable result of violating the law, the fine job we dedicated cops do, and so on.

By the time I completed the citation, I was rather tired of listening to all this drivel. I explained his options, had him sign the ticket, and watched him drive off, still lecturing.

It was one of the strangest traffic stops of my career.

50

IT TAKES AN EXPERT

"LET ME GO!" the man shrieked, struggling to break free. Although he had the desperate strength of the true psychotic, the four of us were stronger. We had him so completely wrapped up, he could barely move. "Get the cuffs on him," Hightower gasped. I was certainly in favor of this, but at the moment I was in no position to help. I was lying across the guy's legs doing my best to hold him down, but it was like riding a bucking horse.

Charlie Suarez had managed to cuff one of his arms, and now the fight was on to get the other one restrained. "Pull his arm over," Suarez yelled. That arm was currently in the care of Deputy Leamon Reaves, who outweighed the guy by at least fifty pounds. Still, he had to strain mightily to get the arm to move, so stoutly did the guy resist.

Reaves and Suarez forced the arm toward the cuffs and, with one final surge, snapped the handcuff on him. As the metal tightened, the man let out a despairing wail. The battle was over.

Exhausted, we lay there for a moment, trying to catch our collective breaths. Finally, Hightower stirred and said weakly, "Gee, fellas, that was fun. Let's do it again."

The original call had been Hightower's. He was to check out a suspicious person wandering in and out of traffic on a busy thoroughfare. He arrived to find a slightly built man standing in the median strip of the divided highway, ducking and flinching as cars hummed by. Hands clamped over his ears, he kept yelling, "Make them stop! Make them stop!" as the cars passed.

I drove up just in time to see the guy shove Hightower and break into a shambling run. David brought him down with a flying tackle, and the fight was on. I jumped in, but quickly discovered the guy was more than a handful. Suarez and Reaves arrived, and soon we were all rolling around in the dirt.

I followed Hightower to the county hospital, expecting more trouble, but the guy was quite docile and willingly got out of the car at the emergency entrance. We walked him inside and placed him in one of the patient cubicles to wait for the psychiatrist.

He sat quietly but every so often would flinch and mutter, "Stop it."

The third time it happened, I asked, "What's wrong?"

He looked up and said, "Lasers."

"Lasers?"

"Yeah, they're beamed at my head, and they hurt."

Hightower rolled his eyes and twirled one finger at his temple. I was a little put off by this somewhat crude display. Granted, the guy was far from normal, but I saw no reason to ridicule him simply because he was mentally disturbed. I was no doctor, but he seemed to be some kind of delusional psychotic, perhaps even schizophrenic. "Who's beaming the lasers at you?" I asked.

He glared at me. "You ought to know."

I kept my voice friendly. "But I don't know; that's why I'm asking."

He looked around the cubicle, as though checking for other people, and finally said quietly, "It's the feds."

"The FBI?"

"Yeah, I think so."

"What do they do?"

He raised his manacled hands and rubbed his head. "They shoot lasers at me; I can feel them in my brain."

"Why?"

He looked around again, then whispered, "So they can control my thoughts, and it makes me mad."

"I don't blame you; I'd be mad, too."

Hightower stared at me, but I ignored him. I sensed I was making progress. "I guess that puts you under a lot of stress."

"Yeah, it does." He tapped the side of his head, and the handcuffs tinkled softly. "Sometimes I feel like I'm going to explode."

"Have you even seen a doctor about it?"

"Yeah, plenty of times." He shook his head. "They don't do me any good; they just give me medicine."

"Do you take it?"

"Not any more," he said emphatically. "It made me crazy."

"ARE you crazy?"

He looked puzzled. "I don't think so, but I'll tell you one damn thing."

"What's that?"

"If they don't stop shooting these lasers at me, I'm gonna go crazy sure enough!"

The staff psychiatrist arrived, and David and I stepped out of the cubicle so he could examine his patient.

"You talk to him pretty good, Don," Hightower said, chuckling. "You related?"

"No, David, I'm not related. All I was trying to do was determine the nature of his illness."

"I'll tell you what's wrong with him. He's a nut, he's loony." He laughed. "I like to died when you started agreeing with him. Did you believe that crap about the lasers?"

"No, I did not," I said loftily. "I was merely trying to draw him out a little, to find out exactly what kind of delusion he was afflicted with."

"Well excuse me, Doctor Parker. The next time I'll show a little more respect."

"Personally, I think he's a paranoid schizophrenic."

IT TAKES AN EXPERT

"Your mother was a paranoid schizophrenic."

Further conversation was ended as the doctor emerged from the cubicle. He wrote busily on the chart while we waited in respectful silence. He completed his entry and headed for the nurse's station.

"Excuse me Doctor," I said. He turned. "Could I ask what your diagnosis is?"

He shrugged. "You got me." He twirled his index finger at his temple. "He's just a nut, I guess." He hurried off, while I stood there, my cheeks flaming and Hightower's raucous laughter ringing in my ears.

51

WHAT THE WELL-DRESSED DEPUTY WEARS

I pulled into the parking lot and stopped. The store specialized in clothing for large ladies. Surely they would have a pair of shoes that would fit me. I hoped so, because time was getting short. When I agreed to do the skit for the Christmas party, I didn't give much thought to where all the parts of the costume were going to come from.

The wig was no problem, I borrowed one from my sister-in-law. My wife found a suitable dress at the Good Will store for a few bucks. She had plenty of makeup. Now all I needed was the high heels, and my outfit would be complete.

But that had been a problem. I couldn't easily borrow a suitable pair of shoes. I had discovered that men's shoe sizes and women's shoe sizes were not the same. The equivalent woman's shoe was two sizes larger than the same size in a man's shoe. I wore a 9 1/2 but I didn't know too many ladies with size 11 1/2 feet.

The place was fancier than I thought it would be. A smartly dressed grandmotherly type approached me. "May I be of assistance?"

Right away I knew I was in trouble. In the cheap places they say "Can I help you?," or "What do you want?," or "You'll have to give us a blood sample before we'll take your check." In the expensive places they say, "May I be of assistance?"

224

WHAT THE WELL-DRESSED DEPUTY WEARS

"Yes, I'd like to get a pair of shoes, black heels, size 11½ D."

Her eyes widened slightly, but she recovered quickly. "Of course, sir, is this a gift?"

"Uh, no. They're for me."

She stared at me, and I added hastily, "It's okay, I'm a deputy."

"A deputy," she repeated.

"Right," I fished my badge case out of my back pocket and flipped it open. We both stared at the photo ID and the slightly tarnished badge. I was getting nervous, and when I get nervous, I don't think straight. Telling her I was a deputy made very little sense. I forced a smile. "Actually, being a deputy has nothing to do with it. You see, I'm going to be wearing the shoes at a party where I'm going to dress up like a woman."

Her eyebrows rose slowly until they were halfway up her forehead, and I felt the first drops of sweat break out on my upper lip. "It's an office party," I said quickly, "There'll be a lot of deputies there."

"Will they all be dressed as women?" she asked.

"Certainly not; what kind of people do you think we are?"

I could tell by the expression on her face what kind of person she thought I was. "I'm sure we can find something in your size," she said, heading toward the back of the store. I followed, cursing myself for not explaining things better. She pulled some chunky black pumps off a display rack. "Are these all right?"

They weren't exactly glamorous, but I was after safety, not fashion. "They look okay, how much?"

"These are 95," she said smoothly.

"Dollars?" I choked. She nodded. "What's the cheapest shoes you sell?"

"Around $50, and those would be sandals."

I felt queasy. "Thank you very much for your time, but I can see I'm in the wrong store."

She smiled, "I thought that from the first."

I drove off, trying to think of a place where I could buy a pair of cheap black heels in a size that would fit. Telling the sales person I was a deputy sheriff was a mistake I wouldn't make again.

A few minutes later, I came upon a bargain shoe store which catered to people with smaller pocketbooks. It was a store I knew well because of their problems with grab-and-run shoplifters. Hardly a day went by that they didn't call us for help. Employees were hired for their size and speed, as much as for their selling ability.

I wandered the aisles looking for something suitable. The prices were quite reasonable, and most shoes were under $20. I finally found some black shoes with a small but solid heel, about an inch in height. There were a multitude of straps, which indicated it should have adequate support. I looked around, but the aisle was deserted. I placed one shoe on the floor and put my shoe next to it. It seemed like a good match, but I had to be sure. They retailed for $14.95, and I wasn't going to lay out that much money for something that didn't fit.

I checked the aisle once more. I was still alone. I slipped off my shoe and stripped off my sock. I got the straps buckled and took a few tentative steps. Even with the minuscule heel, the shoe was alarmingly unsteady. I hoped I wouldn't cripple myself when I wore them in the skit, since I had to prance around the stage while the sheriff and I sang a song.

I took a few more steps, wavering and wobbling. It wasn't too bad. A little practice and I should do all right. I pulled up my pant leg so I could see the shoe, and it was at that moment I became aware I was no longer alone. I looked up and saw a rather large elderly lady looking back at me. I must have made quite a sight, standing there in the aisle, wearing one ladies' shoe, holding my sock and shoe in one hand, tugging on my pant leg with the other, limping along like some sort of demented queen of the May.

I let go of the pant leg as she watched me solemnly. "I'm going to a party," I said, lamely, as if this explained everything.

She nodded. "The shoes are for my mother; she's been quite sick and can't get out too much, so I buy her clothes for her." She nodded again. I scrabbled at the straps, but the damn things wouldn't come loose. I finally got the shoe off and started putting on my sock. She watched my every move, and I felt more self-conscious by the second. "Actually, she's crippled, and I have to do everything for her." I was babbling now, saying anything. I finished dressing, snatched up the shoe box, and almost sprinted for the checkout counter.

Once in line, I calmed down. My explanation may have been a little strange, but it seemed to satisfy the woman. As I waited I could hear snatches of conversation from the people around me. Mothers admonishing children, a young couple discussing their upcoming wedding, and the rather loud voice of an older woman talking to a companion. "That's him up there, with the glasses," I heard her say. "He told me he buys all his mother's clothes for her."

The other voice said, "I wish my son would just call me once in a while."

"His mother's a cripple," the first woman said. "But do you know he's going to have a party for her?"

"The only time my son is going to give me a party is at my funeral."

"Well, I just think it's wonderful. He even tried on her shoes to see if they'd fit."

I paid for my purchase as quickly as I could and left the store, glad I had restored one woman's faith in humanity.

52

THE BOTTOMLESS PIT

It was a shining spring afternoon. The air crisp and cool, the temperature in the sixties and a light wind to stir newly budded branches. It was the kind of spring day I remembered from my boyhood in New York, with winter finally on the run and a few muddy patches of slush the only reminder that snow had once cloaked the ground.

But those days in Westchester County, New York, came in March or April; this was late February. Just one of the benefits of living in the south. Winters are a little easier down here. We don't get much snow in Florida. The largest amount I can remember occurred during the blizzard of '73, when almost an inch and a half of the white stuff literally paralyzed the entire county.

We may not get much snow, but we get plenty of rain, particularly in the spring. We had just endured three full days of it, and I was happy to see the sun. The ground was like a wet sponge because of the deluge, but at least the roads were dry.

It was just before noon when I got the call. "109?"

I picked up the microphone. "Go ahead, I'm on Pine Forest Road."

"10-4. The highway patrol doesn't have anyone available. Assist at a signal 30 on Interstate 10 near the Alabama line, until a trooper is available.''

I acknowledged the call and swung around, flipping on the siren and blue lights. A signal 30 was a wreck with injuries, and I would be expected to render what aid I could until the ambulance got there. I wouldn't actually investigate the accident. That was for the highway patrol. Many years ago we had reached an agreement with them that we would investigate crimes, and they would handle wrecks.

In all my years with the county, I had never worked a single wreck, which was fine with me. I had no desire to handle complicated traffic accidents with multiple vehicles, multiple passengers, and multiple violations. Give me a good old family disturbance any day. For one thing, they didn't last long. Even with an arrest, I could usually finish it up inside an hour. Really complex traffic accidents can take days to work.

I turned onto the interstate and headed west, arriving at the scene within a few minutes. It didn't look too bad. One car was resting in the median, damaged on the left side, and another was on the far side of the highway, one fender crumpled. The injuries must not have been too serious, judging from the size of the crowd. A bad wreck would have drawn spectators like a football game.

The wreck had actually occurred in the eastbound lane, which meant I was on the wrong side of the highway. I slowed and turned across the median, intending to pull in behind the cars. I never made it. Once off the pavement, I felt my cruiser sinking. Softened by the rain, the median was actually a quagmire, camouflaged by grass. Desperately, I accelerated, but my wheels just spun freely, digging me even more deeply into the mud. When it became obvious that I wouldn't be going anywhere, I left the car and went to see about the injured people.

Luckily, the injuries were relatively minor. One driver had a cut on his head, but he was conscious and walking around, and the bleeding was under control. A passenger in the other car was hobbling on a badly swollen ankle. I asked for an ambulance and a wrecker.

Blue lights in the distance told me another cop was arriving. It was a deputy from my shift coming to assist. He saw my bogged-down cruiser car, and I could see him laughing as he turned onto the grass. I started to tell him to avoid the median, but after seeing him laugh at me, I decided that experience is the best teacher. His smile vanished as his wheels sank into the ooze. He, too, tried to drive out, and he, too, was as unsuccessful as I had been.

Redfaced, he left his car and joined me directing traffic. "Why the hell didn't you tell me the ground was so soft?" he said in a strained whisper.

I smiled, "You're a big boy. I thought you could figure it out for yourself. Besides, I wanted the company."

"Thanks a lot, buddy."

"Don't mention it. I was happy to help."

The ambulance was on the scene quickly. Too quickly. Since the injuries were minor, they didn't use their siren, and we were too busy insulting each other to notice its arrival. Before we could stop him, the driver started across the median. For a second, I thought he was going to make it. The tandem wheels on the heavy ambulance really chewed up the ground, and the big vehicle lurched forward, pushing a bow wave of mud ahead of it, but it was all for naught. 30 seconds later, the ambulance joined our two cruiser cars parked in formation, completely helpless.

The crew picked their way through the mud, carrying their first-aid kits. While they waited for another ambulance to arrive, they treated the two injured people and tried to ignore our smirks.

I heard the throaty roar of a big engine and saw the highway patrol trooper coming down the road. I really wanted him to bog down to his hood ornament, but he took one look at our vehicles and wisely decided not to chance the median strip. To our vast disappointment, he parked on the side of the interstate instead.

At last, the wrecker arrived. The driver parked behind the trooper's patrol car and got out.

"You fellas need a little help?" he asked, smiling.

"Yeah," I said, "we could use a little help. Why don't you pull the ambulance out first so he can take the people to the hospital."

He gave me a mock bow. "Your wish is my command."

"Very amusing, but let me tell you something."

"I'm all ears, chief."

I pointed to our muddy and forlorn cars. "You better go up to high ground before you try to cross."

He laughed. "Don't you worry your shiny head about me. This truck ain't no cream-puff poleece car." He swung up into the cab, revved his engine, and started across, mud fountaining from his rear wheels. Just like the ambulance, he made good progress at first, but, to my intense delight, the back wheels began sinking, and the vehicle slowly came to a stop. Cursing, the driver stepped out of his thoroughly mired wrecker and went to his knees in the goop.

It made an interesting sight. Two sheriff's department cruiser cars, one ambulance and a wrecker. All stuck in the mud. The crowd was growing fast, but no one was looking at the wrecked cars. They all wanted to see the immobile emergency vehicles.

We got out eventually. Another ambulance took away the injured. Another wrecker pulled out the stuck one, and the two of them pulled the rest of us free. As the last mud-stained vehicle was winched onto the pavement, the crowd broke into a ragged cheer.

53

GIT ALONG, LITTLE DOGIES

I had just been dispatched to handle a report of livestock loose on a highway, and I was none too happy with the call. I don't like dealing with animals or wives. They're unpredictable and always potentially dangerous.

I was familiar with the property in question. It was surrounded by one of the most rickety fences I have ever seen. Consisting of a few meager strands of rusting barbed wire wound around an occasional fence post, the fence was so laughably inadequate, it was hard to believe it would hold a hamster, much less a full-grown cow. But it did. At least, most of the time. Still, animals would get out every so often and cause traffic accidents.

Once, a particularly feisty steer managed to escape and staked out a choice section of highway. When an eighteen-wheeler came barreling down the road, the steer refused to move. The end result, while somewhat messy, was certainly spectacular and made even more memorable when someone discovered one of the horns of the late steer embedded in the grill of the semi. I hoped I wouldn't face a repeat of that episode.

I arrived, and my headlights illuminated two good-sized calves standing in the middle of the road. I blipped the siren, and they turned tail and scampered off the road. So far, so good.

They headed down a long driveway which dead-ended at the

front gate of a fertilizer plant. "Gotcha!" I said gleefully, as the animals milled around in confusion. I turned my car sideways so I could keep them hemmed up. I kept about twenty feet of rope in the trunk for towing cars, and with visions of rodeos dancing in my head, I fashioned a crude loop and advanced upon the animals.

They rolled their eyes nervously, and I suddenly became aware of just how big these particular calves were. They certainly weighed several hundred pounds each, and the knobs of future horns protruded from their heads. I wondered what my body would look like if I got caught in a two-calf stampede.

But I had a job to do. I threw my makeshift lariat at the closest calf, and a terrible thing happened: The loop went right over its head. That panicked the animals, and they bolted. The rope seared through my hands, and I let go with a yelp of pain. The calves hit the fence, reversed course, and charged right at me! Although I have no recollection of it, I found myself perched high atop my cruiser car as eight hooves thundered past; my ineffectual rope trailing in the dust.

They couldn't go anywhere. My car had them blocked, so they just ran in circles. I was still sitting on the roof, blowing on my burning hands, when approaching headlights announced the arrival of the animal control officer. He was driving a mud-stained pickup and towing a livestock trailer.

He got out, smiling broadly, a large chew of tobacco bulging in one cheek. "Boy, whatinhell you doin' up there?"

Suddenly aware of how ridiculous I looked hugging my blue lights, I climbed down with as much dignity as I could muster under the circumstances.

"Just trying to keep an eye on these animals," I said, "didn't want them to escape."

He spotted the rope trailing on the ground behind one of the calves. "Well, I'll be dogged. You trying to be a cowboy or something?"

I blushed. "Well, no. I, uh, just, uh, thought it might make it easier for you if I lassoed them first."

He shook his head, laughing raucously. "If that don't beat all. You tryin' to take my job away from me, boy?" I didn't reply.

In short order, he herded the calves into the trailer and closed the door. Handing me my pathetic little rope, he asked, "You gonna join the rodeo now?"

"No, I think I'll just concentrate on writing traffic tickets to drivers of speeding pickups."

"I hope you write tickets better than you rope calves," he said as he drove off, still chuckling.

I left, too, cursing him and the calves. It was three days before I could grip the steering wheel of my car.

54

A JOB WELL DONE

It had been a slow Saturday morning, and I was glad when I got the call dispatching me to a theft at a liquor store. The owner greeted me, obviously very unhappy, and waved me to a chair. "One of my employees stole $3400 from me last night."

"How did it happen?" I asked.

"He was supposed to make the night deposit, but instead he took off with my money. I didn't know it was gone until I opened up this morning."

I assured the man the department would do everything possible to catch the guy. "Oh yeah?" he sneered, "Well, where was the Sheriff's Department last night when this guy was stealing from me? Out writing parking tickets?" I stifled the urge to reply in kind and asked a few more questions, hoping to get a lead as to the man's whereabouts.

"All I know is he's supposed to live in a trailer park, but he doesn't have a car; he doesn't even have a phone." He shook his head, "I never should have hired that deadbeat. He drinks up his money as fast as he makes it."

I tried to feel sympathetic, but it was difficult. I knew this man, and I figured he had hired the guy because he knew he could pay him a few pennies more than minimum wage. I told him to call if he got any more information, and I hit the streets.

YOU'RE UNDER ARREST

The owner said the employee walked to work, so I figured the trailer park had to be within a few miles. Since it was a quiet day, I began checking all the trailer parks in the area. There were plenty of them. I would contact the manager of each park and ask for the man by name. Two hours and six trailer parks later, I found him.

He lived at the Oak Woods Mobile Home Park, about three-quarters of a mile from the liquor store. It was a seedy place, full of rusting, faded trailers, most of them at least 15 years old. The unpaved road was cratered with huge, water-filled potholes, and I cringed as the muddy water splashed on my immaculate cruiser car.

The manager recognized the name immediately and told me my man came in rip-roaring drunk around 4:00 A.M. and had to be helped into his trailer. He assured me the guy was still there. "Hell, he ain't going anywhere. He's gonna have too bad a head when he finally wakes up."

Satisfied I had the guy located, I had the radio room notify the duty investigator who was on call. I parked in a position where I could watch the trailer to be sure my suspect didn't leave. The investigator drove up a short time later, and he was not pleased. Even though he was on call, he didn't like having to come in on a Saturday. When I told him who owned the liquor store, however, his attitude changed immediately, and he became the soul of cooperation.

We walked over to the trailer, and I knocked on the door. There was no response. I knocked harder, and the door swung open. On the couch in the cramped and filthy living room was our man, still sound asleep, an empty whiskey bottle on the floor beside him. I walked over and shook him. It took a long time, but he slowly regained consciousness and sat up. Beneath him were ten and twenty dollar bills, and wads of cash bulged from both pockets. He opened his eyes and focused blearily on my uniform. When he realized who I was, he said, "Uh-oh," and collapsed with a groan.

A JOB WELL DONE

I read the man his Miranda Rights and asked him about the theft. He readily admitted stealing the money and said he did it because he couldn't stand working in the store any longer, because the owner was such a tyrant. As I was putting the cuffs on him, he laughed. "Boy, I'd love to have seen his face when he found out the money was gone. I bet he like to died."

We recovered all but $300 which the guy said he spent buying drinks for himself and his buddies. The investigator told me to go ahead and book the man, and he would notify the owner that we had cleared the case. As I was walking out the door, he slapped me on the back. "That was a damn good piece of police work, Don. I wouldn't be surprised if you got a letter of commendation."

My head swam at the prospect. A letter of commendation! I felt like saying, "Aw, shucks, it was nothing," but I managed to restrain myself. I HAD done a good job, and I certainly could use a letter in my file.

A week later I got a letter, all right. The owner of the liquor store wrote the sheriff complaining about the missing $300 and blaming the department for not catching the thief quickly enough. However, he effusively praised the hard work and dedication of the investigator and asked the Sheriff to see he was commended for his hard work.

My name wasn't even mentioned.

55

WE ALL LOOK ALIKE

It was a quiet neighborhood of older homes and older residents, but there were still plenty of kids and the generations tended to clash occasionally, as generations will do. One particular resident, a cantankerous widow in her 60's, clashed more often than most. She didn't like the kids, and they didn't like her. She was constantly calling the cops for one reason or another, but the reasons were rarely serious. Today, however, the situation was reversed.

Several youngsters had been playing football in the street, and the ball bounced into her yard. Annoyed at the noise, she promptly confiscated the ball. The kids quickly got their parents involved, which resulted in a shouting match with two of the mothers, but she still refused to return the ball. Someone called the law.

I had been there before, and I didn't like dealing with her. She had a nasty personality and was quick to call in complaints if she thought we weren't doing our jobs properly.

I arrived and found a small crowd of outraged parents and bug-eyed kids milling around in the street. The lady was standing in her yard, the football under one arm, hurling verbal brickbats at her tormenters. As I stepped from my car, she concluded her harangue by promising that, if any of them so much as set one toe in her yard, she would have the whole crowd arrested.

I spoke to some of the parents, then went to talk to the woman. She was still standing inside the fence, clutching the football. "You can't come on my property!" she yelled as I started to open the gate. She was correct, of course. I had no legal right to do so.

I closed the gate and decided to take a conciliatory approach. "I'm not going to come onto your property if you don't want me to," I said soothingly, "I just want to solve this problem."

There was a rumble of discontent from the crowd behind me, which I ignored. They wanted me to to start lobbing in the tear gas. "Why don't you just give them the football? I'm sure they'll find some other place to play, right, kids?" I said, turning to the youngsters. They agreed, reluctantly. They were hoping the SWAT team would show up.

I turned back to the woman, my most winning smile fixed firmly in place. "So, what do you say?"

What she said, she said very loudly, and it included a stream of expletives that singed what little hair I had. I hadn't heard language like that since I got out of the Navy. Clearly, this had gone far enough. There was no doubt this constituted disorderly conduct. I started in the gate. "You're under arrest" I said.

"Oh, no, I'm not," she shrieked, running for the porch. I was right behind her and would have caught her had she not whirled and thrown the football at me. I ducked, and that allowed her enough time to get inside and lock the door.

Now what? The crowd was going crazy, hoping I'd shoot the lock off. But this was only a misdemeanor. Maybe two misdemeanors. I could always charge her with assault with a football, but I wasn't eager to have to explain this one in open court. I called for the sergeant.

He arrived, listened to my story, looked the situation over, and told me to get a warrant. At least, with the warrant, I could legally go onto her property. It was still a misdemeanor, and I couldn't kick the door down, but he thought I might be able to talk her into coming out. I was doubtful, but it was worth a try.

It took several hours to obtain the warrant, and when I returned, the crowd had departed. I knocked, and the door opened a crack. I held out the warrant. "Ma'am, I've got a warrant for your arrest."

"A warrant? For what?"

"It's for disorderly conduct, from the incident this afternoon. You'll have to come with me."

She came out, considerably calmer now. "All right," she said in a subdued tone, "I'll go with you; I know I did wrong."

When we were in the cruiser, she said, "I guess I just lost my temper."

I agreed this could easily happen.

"Well, at least you've been very nice, and I appreciate your courtesy," she said. "You're a lot more polite than that other guy who was here this morning."

I was confused. "What guy?"

"That man that thinks he's a deputy," she said, sarcasam dripping from every word, "He's the sorriest excuse for a cop I ever saw."

Then I understood. She had no idea I and the "other deputy" were one and the same. It happens. People see the uniform but not the person in it.

We drove in silence for some moments, then she spoke. "Excuse me?"

"Yes, ma'am?"

"Do you know the name of that other man?"

I stifled a smile. "No, I don't, but I can probably find out."

"I'd appreciate it," she said grimly, "because I'm sure going to call the sheriff about him. He was the rudest cop I've ever seen."

56

THE BIGGER THEY ARE...

The bar is long gone now, but in its day it was a pretty rough place. It was a redneck joint, through and through, and offered only three things: country music on the juke box, cold beer in the cooler, and at least one good fight a night.

It had a variety of different names over the years, but there was just not enough business to support the place. The last time I saw the building, it was a beauty salon.

None of us who worked that area were very fond of the bar. The folks who patronized it seemed to enjoy beating up on deputies as much as they did each other. The fact the place was so far out in the boonies didn't please us, either. If trouble started, a backup could be a long time arriving. And trouble seemed to start there all too frequently. One memorable conflict resulted in three deputies and five patrons being transported to the hospital for repairs.

You can understand, then, why, on this particular night, I was less than thrilled to be dispatched to the bar to handle an unknown disturbance call. Unknown disturbance calls make me nervous, and my nervousness increased by leaps and bounds when I found out where I was going.

Of course, when we have to handle potentially dangerous calls or go to bad places, one or more deputies are sent as backups.

But there was a problem. The other deputy working my district was at the jail booking a prisoner, and everyone else was busy. "We'll get you a backup just as soon as someone gets free," the dispatcher told me.

"Thanks a lot, headquarters." I was on my own.

I pulled into the parking lot, and it seemed peaceful enough, no bodies lying in the dirt, no gunshots, no yelling or screaming. I told the radio room I had arrived and stepped inside. The first thing I saw was a flattened table and mangled chair, which did nothing to bolster my confidence. Against the wall, three scruffy patrons watched me warily. The owner, a slimy little guy who was no friend of the department, was behind the bar looking nervous. No one said a word, but I hardly noticed. I only had eyes for the guy at the end of the bar.

He was, in a word, enormous.

I have seen bigger men: Kareem Abdul Jabbar, Arnold Schwarzenegger, the Incredible Hulk; but not at any bar disturbance I ever handled. This guy was about 6'5" and must have weighed 260 pounds. His massive arms bulged with muscles I didn't even know existed.

He was standing quietly, but he didn't look happy, and that made me unhappy, because I wanted very much for him to like me. There was always the possibility I might have to arrest him. If he decided to actively resist, I would have no choice but to shoot him, and I was afraid this would just make him mad.

No one said a word as I continued my slow progress across the floor. I stopped directly in front of Gargantua. I had to lean back a little to see his face, and what I saw was not encouraging.

I had no idea what to say, but as we stood there perhaps a foot apart, I was horrified to hear my voice, although I had no recollection of giving it an order to speak. "I sure hope you're peaceful," it said, "because if you're not, I'm in big trouble."

There was a sharp intake of breath from the small group behind me, and the other part of my mind, the normal part, wanted to faint.

The monster glared at me for what seemed like an hour, then, incredibly, he started to chuckle. Instantly, the rest of the group joined in.

"Yeah, I'm peaceful," he said, "but I had to throw out a few guys who weren't."

It turned out several intoxicated customers had decided to do battle, and he had stepped in to restore order. His efforts were not appreciated by the participants, and they made the mistake of turning on him. He said he was forced to use sufficient force to overcome their resistance and eject them from the establishment. However, he assured me, no one had been seriously injured.

I was so happy I was going to live, I wouldn't have cared if he had told me he had chopped them into kindling wood. I filled out a short report, shook hands all around, and drove off, thrilled everything had worked out so well.

It was the only time I remember going to that place on a disturbance call that I didn't have to arrest someone.

GLOSSARY

BASIC TERMS FOR PEOPLE

SCUM: A broadly inclusive term for undesirable people with whom a cop has to deal every day. (See *DIRTBAG).*

DIRTBAG: A singular example of *SCUM.* An undesirable person. Frequently, a criminal, or thought to be.

CITIZENS: What *DIRTBAGS* become when it is discovered they are friends of the sheriff.

VOTERS: What *SCUM, DIRTBAGS* and *CITIZENS* become at election time.

METHODS OF OBTAINING INFORMATION

INTERVIEW: The method used to elicit information from a *VOTER.*

INTERROGATION: The method used to elicit information from a *DIRTBAG.*

QUESTION: The method used to elicit information from a *CITIZEN.*

TYPES OF CASES

ACTIVE CASE: Any unsolved case in which the news media takes an inordinate amount of interest.

INACTIVE CASE: Any unsolved case which has been ignored by the news media.

STRONG CASE: A case in which the *PROBABLE CAUSE* appears to be insufficient. Occurs most often at quitting time.

GENERAL TERMS

109: My radio identification number with the Escambia County Sheriff's Department.

ARREST: (Also Pinch, Collar, Nab and Apprehend) One of the things cops do to earn a living.

Good Arrest: An arrest that does not result in a lawsuit or an acquittal.

Bad Arrest: An arrest which does result in a lawsuit, an acquittal, or both.

COFFEE BREAK: A temporary respite from the stressful duties of patrolling. This interval of time is devoted to rest, refreshment, and flirting with gum-chewing, heavily made-up waitresses, most of whom are named Cindi, Debbi, or Randi.

CONFESSION: Admission of guilt made by a *DIRTBAG*.

COP: Slang term for a law enforcement officer. The origins are vague. Some believe it is derived from the term, "copper," applied to policemen who wore copper badges. Others think it is an acronym for "Constable On Patrol," a log book entry denoting the particular constable who was on duty, eventually shortened to *COP*.

CRUISER CAR: A painted police car with emergency lights and siren. Some agencies call them patrol cars, squad cars, or units. When I was driving them regularly they had a life expectancy of about three months.

DEFENDANT: The person believed to have committed the crime. (See also *DIRTBAG* and *SCUM*)

HOMICIDE: A death. May result from foul play, accident, or natural causes.

Excusable Homicide: The term used to describe what happens when a cop accidentally eliminates a *CITIZEN* instead of a *DIRTBAG.*

Justifiable Homicide: The term used to describe what happens when a cop eliminates a *DIRTBAG* with the proper provocation.

HIGH-SPEED CHASE: The dangerous and reckless pursuit of a driver who attempts to elude a pursuing law enforcement officer and something near and dear to the heart of every cop.

INFORMANT: Anyone who supplies cops with information about illegal activities. (See also *DIRTBAG* and *SCUM*)

LENGTHY INVESTIGATION: The term used to explain to reporters how all crimes are solved.

PLAIN VIEW: The condition in which all illegal items were found when a cop did not have a search warrant.

PROBABLE CAUSE: That which would cause an experienced and prudent law enforcement officer to believe that a crime was being committed, was about to be committed, or already had been committed by the person or persons he or she has under observation or in custody. Translated into plain English, it is the reason or reasons to believe a crime has occurred.

POLICE BRUTALITY: A media term to describe the force used by a cop which resulted in a *DIRTBAG* filing a huge lawsuit against a law enforcement agency.

REPORTER: Depending on how the story was written, either a fair-minded, responsible journalist or a radical, bleeding-heart liberal.

ROUTINE PATROL: What all cops were doing when they were involved in a traffic accident. We never say we were ogling a women, fiddling with the radio, or looking in the rear-view mirror to comb our hair.

SUBJECTS: The term used by cops to describe people in their reports. Example: "While on routine patrol, I observed three subjects acting in a suspicious manner."

STATEMENT: Admission of guilt made by a *CITIZEN*.

SUPERVISOR: A job-scared, overly cautious, nit-picker, who stays paralyzed with fear most of the time. It's also what all cops aspire to become.

TRAFFIC CITATION: What is given to a *DIRTBAG* if he violates a traffic law.

TRAFFIC WARNING: Most often given to *CITIZENS* and *VOTERS*.

UNNECESSARY USE OF FORCE: The term used by *DIRTBAG*'s attorney to describe the gentle physical restraint required to take his client into custody.

VICTIM: The person against whom the crime was committed. (See also *CITIZEN* and *VOTER*)

CAROLDON BOOKS

This mini-national conglomerate was named after the founders (Carol, Don; Caroldon. Pretty adorable, huh?), and world head-quarters is in Pensacola, Florida. Feel free to call any time. If they're not in, just leave a message on their answering machine.

CAROLDON BOOKS
1075 Farmington Road
Pensacola, Florida 32504
(904) 474-1407